HERE TODAY. "GOON" TOMORROW

here today.
"goon"
tomorrow

Frank W Payne

Matador
9 Priory Business Park,
Wistow Road, Kibworth Beauchamp,
Leicestershire. LE8 0RX
Tel: 0116 279 2299
Email: books@troubador.co.uk
Web: www.troubador.co.uk/matador
Twitter: @matadorbooks

ISBN 978 1800462 151

British Library Cataloguing in Publication Data.
A catalogue record for this book is available from the British Library.

Printed and bound in Great Britain by 4edge Limited
Typeset in 12pt Minion Pro by Troubador Publishing Ltd, Leicester, UK

Matador is an imprint of Troubador Publishing Ltd

ONE

The storm clouds of war were gathering.

As a five-year-old living and learning on a council estate in south east London, Adolf Hitler might well have been a terminal illness for all I knew. Back in England, we were all awaiting the return of Prime Minister Neville Chamberlain, following his meeting in Germany with the chancellor, Adolf Hitler. Once back in England, he broadcast the news there would be no second World War. Hitler had given his word. His assurance. There would be no war. Later, Hitler reneged on his word and ordered the invasion of Poland. When asked to withdraw his troops, he refused. Leaving Chamberlain with no alternative other than to declare war on Germany. Was he a strong negotiator? I think not. Would Winston Churchill have fared better? I think so. We were not prepared, nor anywhere near ready, for a second World War. Unlike Hitler, who had spent the whole of the thirties preparing himself, his henchmen, army, navy and especially the Luftwaffe, for war. Convincing the might of the German war machine that they were ready and able to take on the whole of Europe. And win. It kicked off in 1939 and ended in 1945. In those six years, Hitler was responsible for the death of countless millions of innocent civilians. Many of them women and children. Far more than those dying through terminal illness. The comparison has stayed with me for many decades.

I was just five when the war began. Eleven when it ended. An exciting adventure for me and the other kids on a south east London council estate. A war that I believed would prepare me for the many battles which lay ahead. Sure, there were things that frightened me and that I did not I fully understand. In time, they became an acceptable part of everyday life. Ask your God to keep you safe when you said your prayers at night. So be it, you were. The war might well go on for ever. Or so it seemed to me, if that's what adults wanted. But what could we kids do, except wait for things to happen. The months crept slowly past and none of the bad things adults said would happen did. The opposite in fact. For us, it was a phoney war which lasted for months.

Sadly, I never got to know my real dad, who died at the age of twenty-eight when I was just four months old. The older I became the less I understood why, within eighteen months, my mother married my step-father and we moved into his small house in Deptford. Thank God, only one of his three children lived at home, his house was so small. He was the youngest son in his early teens. Ted, the eldest son, was a despatch rider in the army. He was captured by the Germans early in the war, whilst serving in Crete. He was released soon after the war ended. I briefly met him once he had arrived back in England. He was well into his first year of freedom. He loved motorbikes and purchased a powerful Vincent Black Shadow. Sadly, there were no witnesses to the accident. Ted was found dead on the road's grass verge. His neck was broken. The Vincent was almost eighty yards away, the engine still running. I met Lilly, my step-father's only daughter, who hardly spoke to her father, at Ted's funeral. My mother thought her a lovely girl, who, we later discovered, disliked her father as much as Gwendoline, my elder sister, and I did. To my knowledge, she never came to Kidbrooke, where, thanks to the local council, we were now living on a large council estate. So here I was, the youngest of a dysfunctional family of seven. Living in south east London during the Blitz. A skinny, but otherwise tough, street-wise kid, who made sure others did what I said or did. Something, which came easily, provided I persevered.

Once the Blitz commenced, like many buildings in London, schools near where we lived suffered considerable bomb damage. The Luftwaffe was relentless, carrying out indiscriminate bombing raids night and day. In a short space of time, a significant number of schools had to close their doors, damaged beyond occupancy. The affect this had on children's education was catastrophic. Like it or not, it was the only way you had the opportunity to attend school for four hours in the morning or afternoon. It was the only way to ensure we were at least partially educated, giving children a chance of passing the revised eleven-plus examination. This decided whether you did or didn't qualify for grammar school, the goal of all caring parents.

Whilst my mother encouraged me all she could, my step-father wasn't even aware that, due to bomb damage, I had changed schools three times in eighteen months. My current school, Henwick Road, was almost three miles from where we lived. As schools go, it wasn't bad. Early Victorian with windows boarded to prevent bomb blasts causing injuries to sitting children. There we sat. From 8.30 till 12.30. Desperately cramming as much learning as is humanly possible in such a short space of time. Few of us experienced days that were not touched by sadness. When gazing around overcrowded classrooms, you could not help but see the empty chairs. It was then you knew who would not be coming to school that day, nor probably any other day. It was then that you knew the victims of last night's random bombing.

Kenny Benge was three days older than me and my best school friend. He had a shock of unruly ginger hair, a broad grin which kept a face full of freckles in their place and the skinniest milk-white legs you ever did see.

And he had the nickname Ginger, which he hated. If he wasn't in trouble with the school's collective of teachers at least weekly, he was failing the education system. For all his sins, he held an affectionate place in each and every teacher's heart, mine too. Try as they might to keep Bengie and I apart, they found, in the name of progress, it was far better we sit together. Giving us one hundred lines apiece as a salve to their conscience. Normally, we would meet at the school gates each morning. We didn't on the morning of 12th December 1943. Bengie was always there first, but on this day he wasn't. The foreboding began when I saw he wasn't there. Today, I could wait no longer. There was still no sign of him as I set off to park my bike. Neither was his bike parked in its customary place alongside mine. The foreboding grew ever stronger as the morning progressed. Especially when his younger brother failed to appear in the playground during morning break.

As soon as my four morning hours of schooling were over, I was furiously peddling the two miles to where Kenny lived. I knew something terrible had happened. Believing he was dead or seriously hurt, the sight that greeted me was hard to believe. Horrendous. The entire row of terraced houses, where the Benges lived, destroyed. Together with neighbouring dwellings far beyond. Flattened or severely damaged. Each and every house reduced to a pile of unrecognisable bricks, mortar and household effects. Those responsible for this total carnage, having long since fled for home. Still, air raid wardens, the fire brigade, neighbours whose homes escaped serious damage, stood on top of the wreckage. Looking and listening intently for any small sign or sound of life. Sadly, there was little. All of Kenny's family were killed as they slept. Many of his neighbours too. As I turned to go home, the tears came crowding in. And the reality of war struck with a vengeance. It was no longer an adventure. It was an adult game with tragic consequences. People were dying because an insane, power-crazed German dictator had decided he wished to rule the world. Ordering the deaths of innocent civilians from the skies.

I thought the war should have ended when Bengie died. It didn't, of course. Everything went on as before but with a remarkable difference, I was always delighted if and when England won anything. Sixty-seven years later, I still am. Since Kenny's death, we were winning the war. With the last throw of the dice, Hitler introduced his new weapons of terror. The first was a jet-propelled flying bomb. The pilotless V-1, controlled from bases in Europe, mainly the Netherlands. Fuelled to fly the shortest route to targets in London and the south east. Once launched, the V-1, fuselage packed with explosives, flew directly to its pre-set target. With little or no fuel left, the flying bomb's engine cut out and it plummeted to earth with no warning. Killing thousands of innocent, unsuspecting civilians. To this day, I never discovered why it was incongruously named 'Doodlebug'.

It was Saturday lunchtime and my mother had just returned from a rare shopping trip to Lewisham. She had been religiously saving her money for the hair perm she had promised herself. As usual, my step-father was fighting the war from his favourite bar stool in the Dover Patrol. The air raid siren had sounded minutes earlier. My mother had just started to prepare lunch, and being busy, decided to ignore the warning and remain in the house. But not this time. She grabbed my hand and screamed at my sister to run for our air raid shelter, some hundred yards or so down the road.

As we raced for our shelter, built during the first year of the war, the doodlebug appeared over the rooftops. I could see flames snarling from the raised rear exhaust. Suddenly, the engine cut out. Just as we reached the entrance to the shelter, it banked, as if caught by an invisible gust of wind and smashed into the middle of the road below. With the strength born of terror, my mother kicked open the shelter door and literally flung us in. I knew she was close behind when the doodlebug's engine stopped. The explosion which followed was awesome, partnered by a blinding flash and a hot, searing wind. My mother, who just seconds before had looked so pretty with her newly permed hair, lay still and unmoving. The lower half of her body under the door, blown off its hinges; her face and upper body bloodied; her perm wrecked. By now, both my sister and I were crying out for help. The front of the shelter had partially collapsed and we were trapped in semi-darkness. After what seemed an eternity, but in truth was only minutes, I thought I could hear shouting. Both Gwen and I were now frantically shouting and screaming back. The voices grew louder. We could hear rubble being moved. Then, through the swirling, acrid debris, dust and smoke, a strong pair of hands appeared as if by magic. The small hole was quickly enlarged and our rescuer could see there were three of us. I was lifted from my mother's body as she regained consciousness. It seems the shelter door hit the back of her head, causing a large cut that was bleeding quite heavily. A dressing was applied and very quickly we were in the ambulance, hospital bound. We were kept in overnight and the following day my mother's brother Cyril collected us. They kept my mother in for forty-eight hours for observation. She was most upset that her perm, less than six hours in place, had been totally ruined. The remnants shaven when the hospital bandaged her head wound.

People died. Derek and Teddy Chamberlain's dad, an ARP warden, was killed bravely directing people to the nearest shelter on the green, just as the doodlebug engine cut out. In all, four people died, including pensioner Mrs Mullins who was standing at her front door, which she did whenever she thought something was happening. Almost all of the houses at the top of the road, ours included, were demolished by the blast from the flying bomb. Had it travelled in the opposite direction, it was likely we could have died too. As for my step-father, he hadn't a clue what had happened.

Even though the pub was less than two miles from the explosion, when he finally left the Dover Patrol and arrived home, he found out there wasn't one any more. Apparently having been told we were amongst the injured taken to hospital, he did nothing except write on the side of our exposed, battered kitchen cupboard, "Bombed, blasted and buggered-up – nowhere to go". Typical of the senseless, useless and undeniably foolish little Irishman that he was.

Four years on, the war had become tiresome. There was a drastic shortage of so many things that were readily available in the peace-time life of a young boy growing up. The continuous day and night time bombing raids were now fewer and further between, replaced by Adolf's growing use of doodlebugs and then the V-2 rocket. The latter being a large, cylindrical, self-propelled rocket loaded to the gunnels with highly explosive material. Like the doodlebug, once the fuel was exhausted, it silently fell from the heavens. There was no defence against it, because you never heard or saw it coming. The resulting death and serious injuries caused were catastrophic. Over three hundred were killed when a V-2 demolished a large Woolworths store and a packed Lewisham shopping centre. Thank God it was not on the same day as my Mum's hair appointment. We also thanked God that England and her Allies were fighting the war in Europe. Luckily, the introduction of the V-2 as a weapon of war was short-lived. Had it been available to Hitler at the start of

World War Two, history would have had a completely different story to tell.

However tough life was then, as a nation we learned to grin and bear it. There were not many of them, but when the brighter moments came along, they were grabbed with both hands. If you are proud to be British, you will know that we were born with street parties in our blood. No matter the constant daily adversities faced, anything beneficial happening within the community and Bingo! It was party time. Out came people's tables and chairs; what food could be spared from the rations available; every conceivable type of home-brewed beer, cider and other hard-to-discern alcoholic beverage, the latter to be handled with care. Then, most important of all, out came the Bunclarks' ancient piano. Propelled by the family from their garden shed to the village green, once in place, up went the chant, "*Vera! Vera! Vera!*"

Vera Hatcher was a veritable enigma, an inch short of five feet tall, apron-clad whenever seen in public, her feet thrust into house slippers so threadbare the dustmen refused to take them away, but glory be! What an unbelievable pub pianist she was. We, her devoted neighbourhood fan club, adored her. She had a playing ability second to none, even though the fingers on both hands were so fat and fleshy they could have graced any butcher's shop window. She had never had a lesson in her life. If you asked for a number she didn't know, you would sing the first half-dozen bars and she was away. I truly love music, singing with male voice choirs for over forty years. Throughout my adult life, I have believed music enters my body through my feet and leaves through my soul. Vera played and, whether you had a voice or not, you sang. The parties went on well into the evening. We had spoon players, solo singers, dancers, ventriloquists, magicians and any number of unfunny comedians. Lilly Lester swore she was once a member of the Bloomsbury Dancers. In her early sixties, she still loved to demonstrate her high-kick routine. Trouble was, being forgetful, the first time she did her routine in front of us boys, she had forgotten to put her knickers on. Forgotten, or on daring purpose? For most, if not all, of us, it was the first time we had a close-up of that part of a woman's anatomy. And it was the last. Before she ever danced again, one of the mums would carry out an exploratory search beneath her skirt.

Early on, when the Blitz was at its heaviest in 1940, the council built a large reinforced communal shelter on the main coastal road. We had an indoor Morrison shelter constructed over the dinner table. We couldn't all get beneath it and knew it provided little shelter from a direct hit or near miss. Nonetheless we used it once the warning siren sounded. Being the smallest, Gwen and I were bundled into the broom cupboard under the stairs, exceedingly uncomfortable. We were scheduled to have our own block of shelters built in the coming months. But not yet. So, night after night we stayed at home, praying we would not be harmed. On this occasion, my mother had a premonition all was not well. Just as soon as the warning siren finished wailing, we were all gathered together and set off for the new, large public shelter on the main coastal road. We three children, Mum and the cat, plus numerous bags of food, drink and clothes. It was as if she expected the Germans to lay siege to the shelter we were in, which was about five-hundred yards from our house. As we were running, we could hear bombs exploding away to the south east. Closer to us, numerous incendiary bombs were falling in clusters, exploding and burning incandescently with bright blue phosphorous flames. That made us gallop ever faster. My step-brother arrived first and swiftly unbolted the door. Now breathless, we burst into the pitch-black shelter interior. Surprise, surprise, there wasn't a soul inside. Almost in unison, eight petrified eyes gazed heavenwards. All we saw was stars. They hadn't put the roof on yet. Later, we could see the funny side of it, but then we were too frightened to leave whilst the air raid continued. Only heading for home when the all clear sounded.

Whilst I believe the air raid wardens must have had a clearly defined role in the war, nobody quite knew what it was. They were known only by the initials ARP. As soon as the air raid siren sounded, they appeared on the streets. If a chink of light was showing through a curtained window, up went the shout, "Put that bloody light out!" But seriously, they did much more. Being outdoors, they were often the first to arrive where dropped bombs had exploded, listening and helping locate buried victims, helping other rescue services fight fires and guiding people to the various air raid shelters close by. Those air raid wardens were brave, brave men.

They were dedicated men, usually too old or unfit to be called up. Not meeting with Chamberlain's request to all men aged eighteen to forty to volunteer to join up, they were out there with the bombs falling, each and every night. I think it was my Uncle Cyril who persuaded my step-father to join the ARP, which he did. They decided to fight fires started by incendiary bombs before they took hold. No sooner had the first wail from the air raid siren sounded than Cyril grabbed his stirrup pump and off he set.

He lived five minutes away, but did it in three. At the same time, my step-father would start to fill his two buckets with water. I stood at the open kitchen door, awaiting Cyril's arrival. As he put his foot on the step, a large piece of exploded shell hit him – fair and square in the middle of his tin helmet, bounced off and landed under the kitchen table. Cyril staggered and fell into the kitchen, just as I was reaching for the piece of shell, which we kids collected and called shrapnel. It was red-hot, having fallen from the atmosphere, and badly burned my hand. Semi-conscious, Cyril fell into my step father and two very full water buckets. Pandemonium ensued as three very wet persons tried to restore order. It would have made a wonderful slapstick sketch, but this was war. By the time order was restored, our valiant fire-fighting crew decided to stay at home, as this particular air raid had practically ended. The remaining aircraft that could, hurriedly turned tail and fled for home. The next morning, the BBC radio reported Winston Churchill had congratulated the RAF for inflicting one of the heaviest enemy bomber losses ever suffered by the Luftwaffe.

Early in the war, and weather permitting, Hitler maintained non-stop day and night bombing raids on selected UK targets. The longest was a ten-hour night-time raid targeting the docks and RAF fighter airfields. You can imagine how busy the ARP volunteers were, Cyril and my step-father included. Off went the air raid siren and off set Cyril, steel helmet tied to his head, stirrup pump strapped to his back, large shielded torch in hand, whistle firmly gripped in teeth. Whilst he was on his way, my step-father was filling his two water buckets so he was ready to go when Cyril arrived at the kitchen door. My part in this nightly ritual was to simultaneously open the kitchen door and switch off the light. We were the Home Front's first line of defence. We had no desire to be an illuminated target for Jerry bombers.

Those street parties helped us grin and bear it. It wasn't easy. Food was scarce and rationed. So were clothes. As for luxuries, had they been affordable, which they weren't, you needed black-market friends to bring the prices down. But, given half a chance, it never stopped us celebrating. Believe it or not, some of those parties ignored close-call raids. Occasionally, during daylight raids, we watched dog-fights. Cheering our Spitfire and Hurricane heroes, as, often outnumbered, they bravely engaged the enemy bombers and fighter escorts. As I said earlier, food rationing set the party mums what seemed to be insurmountable problems. But, whatever the ingredient limitations, they never once let us down. Their innovation was truly magnificent, as they made certain nobody went short. We were also often surprised how those who chose to entertain us, whatever they did, just got better and better, whilst the war went on with no end in sight. Ernie Johnson didn't have to get better, he had a lovely voice from the very beginning. Like Vera Hatcher, who was a musical magician of the keyboard, so Ernie was able to sing any song requested word perfect. Being practically sightless was a great handicap, yet he only needed to hear the song once and it became part of his repertoire. He was in his mid-thirties when, for reasons unknown, he threw himself from his bedroom window during a particularly heavy raid. He survived but was badly injured. On leaving hospital, he was evacuated to a virtually air raid free rural location in Somerset.

Seventy years on, I still remember those street parties with fondness. Indomitable spirit in the face of lasting adversity. In the company of people, the likes of whom I was never to meet again. Memories, which will remain with me forever. The Roxy Cinema, blitzed overnight with just the frontage remaining, hanging from which was a huge banner proclaiming the title of the film now showing: *Gone with the Wind*. Most of it had. The thick, pungent layer of stinking black oil from an oil bomb. Something new that Germany introduced to the war which was supposed to ignite on impact but never did. Break-away barrage balloons chased through the streets by loads of screaming kids. Ceaseless hordes of American convoys, nose to tail, heading for their southern marshalling points ahead of the coming invasion of Europe, escorted by small children offering their sisters in exchange for chocolate or bubble-gum. The incredibly noisy Bofors ack-ack guns being towed, parked and fired when enemy aircraft were caught and held in the fingers of searchlight beams. So many incident-packed memories indelibly engraved on the minds of those youngsters who lived through the London Blitz.

TWO

My education suffered badly because all my lessons were halved. By the time the dreaded entrance exams that would decide my future school came around, having only four hours schooling each day was a serious handicap. Due to indiscriminate bombing, not targeted by the Luftwaffe, many schools were victims, causing damage enough to make them unsafe for occupancy. Consequently, in eighteen months, I received my daily four hours learning in no less than three different schools. Currently, I was receiving my daily dose of the three Rs at Henwick Road School, a three-mile bicycle ride from home. Not being an academic, I already knew my chances of getting the pass mark needed to Shooters Hill Royal Academy was doubtful. Especially knowing it was the most popular choice of school in the area for boys of my age. With just weeks to go before I sat the entrance exams, I was resigned to failure. For the last three weeks, I crammed for all I was worth. What happened next, nobody could have foreseen.

Entrance exam day dawned. By 9.15 a.m., I was sitting nervously at my desk in classroom 14b waiting for the off. All of the windows were taped- or boarded-up as a precaution against bomb blasts splintering window glass into the classroom. At 9.30 a.m., we began the first examination. The silence was uncanny. By 11.30a.m., I was beginning to think the papers I'd finished so far were not so bad after all. Then, without any warning whatsoever, all hell broke loose. The explosion was deafening and most of 14b's ceiling fell on the heads of those below. The V-2 rocket fell silently on the far side of the school playground, some four-hundred yards from where we were doing our level best to achieve examination pass marks. Some of the girls amongst us began to cry, but there was no mass hysteria. Probably because we had endured almost five long years of day and night bombing, our reactions were reserved. What's more, we owed our heartfelt thanks to whoever taped the windows. Most of them held firm and injuries were few and superficial. I think the discipline shown by our teacher in charge stopped what might well have been panic. Mr Thomas was quite new to the school but had already earned the nickname 'Tosser'. Although not one of my regular afternoon teachers, whenever he did teach my class, he constantly prowled the classroom. As he walked back and forth, his right hand never stopped jerking in his right-hand trouser pocket. It was no doubt a nervous habit, but it quickly earned him the name Tosser.

No sooner had the dust and pieces of fallen ceiling plaster settled on the children below than he took a quantum leap in my respect. With gentle but firm control, he brought order to chaos. His voice, full of teacher authority, quickly formed the sitting children into two standing lines. He then marched us out of the stricken classroom, into the long corridor and out onto the playground. It was a sight to behold. This tall, gowned figure, covered in white plaster dust, right-hand jerking madly in right-hand pocket, leading two rows of dust-covered examinees onto the playground, where, awaiting them, were members of the emergency services and a sprinkling of panicking parents. It must have seemed a strange spectacle to them, this white-covered spectre followed by two lines of equally white-covered children. All of them well and truly plastered. Thanks to Tosser's swift action, none of us were seriously injured and those with cuts and bruises were quickly ambulanced to hospital. Neither seen nor heard, the damage caused by the V-2 meant that Henwick Road School, so seriously damaged, never opened its doors again. Nor were we ever asked to complete the rest of the entrance examination.

I just could not believe my luck. The papers I had practically completed first were subjects in which I should do well. And I did. It was then decided the marks given to them by the examiners would be used to select not only the successful entrants, but also the new schools they would attend. Not only was I convinced that I would never pass the entrance exam, but even if by some miracle I had, I never once thought I would be considered for Shooters Hill Royal Academy. The very best school for miles around. How gobsmacked was I when I realised the most hated man in Europe had made it all possible. *Danke*, Adolf.

Growing up in war-torn England taught me not to make too many resolutions. It also taught me many other things: respect, assertion, fighting for your beliefs, never a loser be, the truth cannot lie. But I wasn't prepared for battles I was destined to lose. Some of which I did, later in life, with traumatic consequences.

THREE

No sooner had the letter arrived confirming I had been accepted by Shooters Hill, my mother went potty. She made it her crusade to notify all of her rather large circle of neighbourhood friends and associates of her son's achievement. Before I knew it, I was becoming a local hero. A Kidbrooke council estate celebrity. It didn't go as far as autographs, but being congratulated on the street by people I didn't know was a new experience. I almost began to believe I had done something laudable. On the other hand, it proved to be quite helpful when it came to a very long list of school disciplines. It was a comprehensive list of dos and don'ts, compiled since the year dot. "Sod it," I thought. "This is going to be my Achilles heel." But then, as the new term hadn't yet started, I wasn't yet a Shooters Hill "ringworm". So I could, if I wished, turn down the invitation. Then again, if I did so, it would break my mother's heart. And I would never knowingly do that. Especially as she was already asking her closest friends if she could borrow some of their clothing coupons. Enabling me to be properly dressed in the school uniform on my first day as a Shootershillian.

Whilst I wasn't quite sure about the school, I was most definitely certain about the school uniform. It was horrible. Whoever designed it had a violent hatred of schoolboys. Perched upon your head was a hideous cap, black with yellow and green bands, hence the name "ringworm". No doubt coined long ago by a local, it had to be worn at all times when outside of school premises. Next came the blazer, black with a large yellow badge on the breast pocket. The blazer was to be worn at all times, unless given a master's permission to remove it. Beneath it was a grey shirt and knotted black-and-yellow striped tie. But the worst was yet to come. All pupils below the age of thirteen had to wear short trousers. I hadn't worn short trousers for months and months and I had no intention of ever wearing them again. The whole idea, should I comply with the order, was belittling. But, yet again, as a Shooters Hill pupil, there were no options. So short grey trousers it was. Finally, the socks were full length to the knee, grey with yellow-ringed tops. Not only was the uniform unsightly, it was also expensive. To ensure we could afford it, my mother took a second job on board, adding the task of pub cleaner to the food preparation kitchen help she already provided at the Dover Patrol. Whilst I am no expert in the field of medicine, I am certain that, because of the help and support she so willingly and always gave where I was concerned, it contributed to her early death. She was only fifty-four when she died.

My new school was about five miles from Birdbrook Road. There were no school buses then. Neither did we have a car nor any family member who could drive. Fortunately, another of my mother's brothers promised to buy me a bicycle if I passed the entrance exam. Uncle Sidney was a director of a leading shoe manufacturer. Sadly, the only child they had was seriously brain damaged at birth. His brain never kept pace with his physical growth and didn't develop beyond the age of five. Consequently, he was confined to a wheelchair and lived in a specialist hospital. Sid's wife, Winifred, was, according to my mother, "Very posh but rather nice." I was always told, prior to their visiting us, to speak properly and be on my best behaviour. Each time they came, I did my level best when in their presence and I think I became their favourite nephew. Uncle Sid, delighted with my exam result, arrived one week later, on a Saturday. I was allowed to sit beside him in his Jaguar whilst he drove to Gamages, a large Holborn store in London. I had never been inside a car before. Yet, here I was, a passenger in this mobile opulence, on my way to central London, where I had never been before. I felt heaven blessed. Even more so when I was allowed to choose a James Grose super featherweight bicycle with dropped handlebars. I think I must have thanked Sid and Winnie one hundred times on the way home. Now I would arrive at my new school with bags of style. Not on my hitherto knackered rust bucket of a bike with no mudguards.

The following Saturday we were off once again. Shopping for me. Woolwich this time. But, try as I might, the level of excitement never got beyond zero. Why? Well, might you ask? Accompanied by my mother, having finally reached the expensive, targeted cash and coupon pile, it was for my awful school uniform. Having seen it worn when attending the school's new pupil intake ceremony, trying it on, item by item in a crowded store, was a chore. Looking around at the other first timers in various stages of the Shooters Hill uniform, without exception they all looked equally uncomfortable. Especially when it came to the short trousers which some of them refused to put on. Foolish really, knowing they would have to wear them from day one until they were thirteen.

Local kids hated us. To them we were a bunch of stuck-up, snotty-nosed, yellow-bellied "ringworms". Caught alone outside of school, you were in trouble. The prize they sought was your cap. So when off school limits, you did your best to hide it. But doing so laid you wide open to punishment if seen by prefects or teaching staff. On the other hand, wear it and they would snatch it. Again, leaving you open to school punishment until replaced. So you never went out alone – always mob-handed. Enough of you to ensure they left you well alone. Then again, if your group outnumbered theirs, the locals turned tail and fled. It was great fun putting them to the sword, so to speak.

The discipline was strict. The cane was an everyday threat. Written lines generously given for the most trivial of offences. The punishment we all tried our damnedest to avoid was Saturday-morning detention. Why? Shooters Hill was a rugby playing school, but most of us loved and played football. Many junior matches were played on Saturday afternoons, so many of us played school rugby in the morning, team football in the afternoon. Some, of which I was one, played for Sunday league teams as well. Fine at eleven, not so at fourteen, when playing times grew longer, the opposition grew stronger and injuries happened more often. Something had to give so I gave up Saturday soccer. At Henwick Road School, we had a playground, but at Shooters Hill it was a quadrangle, where at all times you had to walk, never run. If caught doing so you were reported by prefects to the duty master and given a minimum of two hundred lines. Because of overcrowding at Henwick Road, the gymnasium was converted into temporary classrooms. Here, they were magnificently equipped. Every piece of kit was lovingly worshipped by an ogre of a PE master. Upset him and you were subjected to thirty minutes of physical torture, commencing with twenty-five press-ups.

Throughout my four years at Shooters Hill, I remained academically average. Virtually every half-

and full-term report said the same thing, 'Needs to pay more attention and try harder.' I did, but only in those subjects dear to my heart. They did not include algebra, geometry, physics, woodwork and Latin. Especially Latin, which I considered a language of medicine and religion. Neither of which had career interests for me in future life. Whereas English, history and, to a lesser extent, geography held my full attention. I also enjoyed physical education, where I was considered a bit of a star and captained the junior school team.

Because so many houses were flattened in the continuous day and night German bombing raids, empty houses were requisitioned by the government. As our house in Birdbrook Road was all but demolished when the doodlebug dropped in for lunch, we were moved into one such empty house. It was situated two miles on from where we had been living on the main coastal road. Our new address was 145 Rochester Way, Blackheath. Compared with our previous small council house, this was twice the size and sheer domestic opulence. For my step-father, it was a dream come true. He now lived directly opposite the Dover Patrol, his local. Drunk, he could roll down the steps, across the car park and main road, and onto the front lawn of the new house. It was while living there that the back gate was left open. Probably by the milkman. Floss, my dog and the love of my life, wasn't going to miss this heaven-sent opportunity to explore her new territory. She disappeared, only to reappear, three months later in the most unexpected of places.

FOUR

It was my third year of learning and it seemed as though every lesson was intent on giving me a hard time. Some much harder than others. So much so that those I disliked from the beginning, I now hated with a vengeance. As a working journalist, where on earth would I be called upon to use Latin, algebra, logarithms. Whatever logic I applied to these and other lesser-liked subjects, the answer was a lemon. So surely it stands to reason. When they became live, my brain went dead. And stayed dead for the duration of the lesson.

In each of my annual school reports, which only my mother ever read, those teaching my list of hated subjects wrote virtually the same thing, "Shows little or no interest in this subject." I know she was not happy and found it hard to accept my explanation. She was even more upset when I told her I was seriously thinking of leaving school as soon as I reached fourteen years of age, less than a year away. Whilst I could never be sure, Mr Elliot, my English and history teacher, tried very hard to encourage my career ambitions. He said he was very pleased with my yearly progress in both subjects, especially English. The content and composition of my written essays showed great promise, full of wild imagination and colourful prose. He read them all with great interest. It was him, over everybody else, who helped me decide I would become a journalist.

Having decided to leave Shooters Hill Academy, none of my school friends would know until I was on my way. The right decision as it happened. Three months earlier, I was heartbroken when Floss, my dog, disappeared. We were living in our requisitioned house at that time. The house was on a major road, consequently, it was busier than most. So I hung a notice on the back-garden gate, reading, "Please shut the gate. Dog loose in garden". On this particular morning, somebody didn't. From the moment Floss entered the house, a curtain of mistrust developed between the two dogs. Trying to keep them apart wasn't easy.

Returning from school, my mother tearfully told me Floss had gone missing. The tears came easily and I immediately grabbed my bike and set off in search of my beloved Floss. This became a regular after-school intensive three-week search, but to no avail. I even involved school mates with the promise of five cigarettes as a reward for whoever found or had sight of her. I now believed her dead. But she wasn't, as months later we were reunited. And, believe it or not, it was Floss who found me.

One of the boys who followed me from Henwick Road to Shooters Hill was Arthur Ayley. I suppose you would call him more of a nodding acquaintance than a friend. He was tall, very slim with girly features. "A girl in a boy's body" was a description which suited Arthur admirably. We were poles apart. He was clever, very clever. And, as I was soon to find out, he liked me. Something I was able to use to my advantage. Whenever my set homework was either too much or too long, or more often than not, both. He wasn't a smoker. Just as well, as I called upon his help quite a bit and, had he smoked, using his services so often, my limited supply of renegade cigarettes would have rapidly disappeared.

Arthur was the fall guy for everybody's jokes. Some of them beyond the pale. At the beginning, I was one of the offenders, but when boys in the class ran a competition as to whom could debag Arthur the quickest that was enough. He was kind and gentle and not deserving of such rough treatment. By threatening to report everyone involved, I made sure it never happened. Arthur was extremely grateful. In fact, I was the only one who lost his trousers in punishment for spoiling the others' fun. It was then I decided school time was over. I would leave on my next birthday when I would be fourteen. I needed my mother's approval and it would be most difficult persuading her. Unless of course I had a job to go to. My career desire was to become a sports journalist on a national newspaper.

These were my continuing thoughts when it happened. I knew very little about the Mason twins, other than rumours that they were a couple of young toughies who were running a successful shoplifting business in the Woolwich branch of Woolworths. They were in the same year, but different classes. When I asked Alan Conroy about the rumour, he said it was no rumour but a thriving business. One they had been running regularly for some months now. Each time their stationery order book for those in the know was full, whichever brother's turn it was would visit the Woolwich Woolworth store and fulfil the order list. Meanwhile, the other brother would explain to his form master why his twin would be late for school. They would only steal the required items to order. Items they could easily conceal on their person and in their school satchels. Alan asked if I wanted anything on the next trip and I said I would give it some thought and let him know. Thank God I never did. Bernard Mason was caught bang to rights stealing items. This time they were items he wanted for himself, items of jewellery intended to impress the new girl who had recently moved into his street. His luck had finally run out.

Having visited Woolies often, the brothers Mason knew every store detective employed to protect the large store from shoplifters, or so Bernard thought. As ever, those the brothers knew they were easy to avoid when working, as he completed his stationery haul. So he moved to the jewellery counter, ignoring the woman viewing the cosmetic counter close by. To date, the Woolwich branch of Woolies had never employed a female store detective. Now, with the opening of a fashion division, this had changed. The lady concerned moved closer to Bernard and watched him pocketing various pieces of jewellery. Then, walking to the entrance ahead of Mason, she confronted him as he reached the store's large front doors. Introducing herself, she asked him to accompany her to the manager's office. Within moments, the manager's desk was covered by a multitude of small stationery items and cheap jewellery. Bernard the Bold soon became Bernard the Blabber. For all but one of his list of clients were his school customers and the manager called the school. In no time at all, the school headmaster had joined the already crowded small office.

When he received the call, Taffy Affleck persuaded the Woolies manager to do nothing till he arrived. As members of the same lodge, they knew each other well. Well enough for the manager to accept Mr Affleck's guarantee of the severe punishment he would announce at tomorrow's assembly. He even invited him to attend. An invitation, which was politely refused. Letters to all parents of those involved were duly sent, in tandem with the cane administered by the head to all pupils on Mason's list. This he did in front of the whole school. As for the Masons, they too suffered six strokes of the cane and were expelled. My departure date from school was now fast approaching and I had told no one. My desire to become a journalist remained my boyhood dream.

FIVE

Do you believe in miracles? No, nor do I. That was until a cold, rainy, very miserable mid-afternoon in mid-November. Piggy Prothero was droning on about the value of Latin in modern-day society. Just fifteen more minutes of his brain-numbing garbage and I would be set free. My gaze returned to the window overlooking the gently sloping lawns. Dusk was almost upon us when I thought I saw a strange shadow on the horizon. I looked long and hard as it assumed a dog-like appearance. I looked away, then back. The apparition was still there. Dare I believe it, it seemed to be moving nearer. Then close enough to dispel all doubt. It was a dog – a very wet, bedraggled, skinny dog. Close enough to be recognised and less than fifty yards from me. I kept looking, but now there were no longer doubts. It was a dog. A long-lost dog. A dog by the name of Floss. It was my missing dog.

Momentarily, insanity banished reason. I cut short Prothero in his Latin prime and I was on my feet shouting, "Sir, it's my dog! It's my dog! I must take her home! Please sir, she's been missing for a long time. I thought she was dead." By the time I had reached the classroom door, I was in shock. Shouting and screaming "Floss!" over and over again. Prothero's voice was fast fading as I raced down the long first-floor corridor. Then down the stairs and out through the double doors. Once outside, there could be no doubt. Tail wagging furiously and barking incessantly. As I held Floss in my arms I realised just how pitifully thin and bedraggled she was. Her condition brought tears to my eyes. Suddenly, Mr Prothero was standing beside me. Being so overweight, he was totally breathless and could hardly speak and I was frightened he would collapse. But there was no way I would let Floss go. Especially as the moment he appeared, Floss growled menacingly. The ringing of the bell announced school had ended. I knew I was in trouble. A lot of trouble. So I removed my school tie, slipped it through Floss's collar, which remarkably had remained around her neck, and I set off for home, apologising to Mr Prothero as I started to run with Floss safely anchored by my side.

Floss trotted happily with me. Apart from her pitiful condition, it was as if she had never gone missing. My mother was in the kitchen and when they saw each other they both went mad. Mum was alternately crying and laughing whilst Floss raced round and round the kitchen. She only stopped when she no longer had the strength to wag her tail. That was when I realised I had no idea when she last ate.

As she tucked into the remainder of the last of the weekend joint – it was supposed to have been our dinner – I told Mum what had happened. Like me, she could not believe that Floss had actually found me. There and then she said she would write to the headmaster, explaining just how much Floss had meant to all of the family, especially me. How long and hard we had searched for her. That was all except my step-father who I still maintain was responsible for her disappearance. She also explained how I was intending to leave school on my fourteenth birthday. I left the letter with the headmaster's secretary. My heart was pounding when he announced he wished to see me in his office after assembly. How deeply I was in trouble I could only guess. But I was convinced I was in over my head. A very stern voice greeted my timorous, almost apprehensive knock on his office door and I entered, terrified. I left no longer believing he was unable to forgive sinners their sins. I had never been confronted by the head in his office before. He sat me in the only chair and he sat on the edge of his large, highly polished oak desk. His eyes never left my face. Finally the silence was broken.

"Thank your mother for her letter. She has explained just how much your dog meant. Not only to you, but your whole family. Whilst I understand, I can't condone your behaviour. You were forbidden to leave the classroom, which you totally ignored, and you called Mr Prothero 'Piggy', which was extremely rude. If the circumstances had been different, you would have been expelled. However, as your mother's letter informed me you wish to leave this school at the end of term, I've decided instead to give you five hundred lines and a Saturday-morning detention in which to do them. Finally, during morning break, you will find Mr Prothero and apologise. You are dismissed, but news of any further misdemeanours and you will be expelled. Immediately. Do you understand?"

For my remaining time at school, my behaviour was impeccable. Even though it was against all I stood for, I really worked hard on those subjects I hated. So much so it was reflected in my last school report. Even Piggy – sorry, I couldn't resist it – made comment upon how much my work had improved.

— SIX —

Fortune favours the brave.

I had no misgivings when I said farewell to Shooters Hill Royal Academy. My mother did and we argued for hours. She tried her level best to persuade me to stay on for just one more year and she only stopped when I showed her my letter of appointment from the *Sunday Pictorial*. Today known as the *Sunday Mirror*. Unbeknown to her, I had written to four different national newspapers, seeking employment as a junior reporter. Only one replied, asking me to attend an interview two weeks later at their then London offices in Geraldine House, Fetter Lane, Fleet Street.

As delighted and excited as I was, I decided to tell no one. I knew how proud my mother would be when I produced the *Sunday Pic* letter – it would go into her handbag to be produced at every conceivable opportunity, even to people she hardly knew. When my step-father found out, he told me that despite my fancy education, the best job I could expect was that of 'go-for'. He then took great delight in colourfully explaining what useless objects go-fors were. I politely thanked him for telling me and added that it described his job to a tee: every day, six days a week, collecting shillings from gas meters, hopes of promotion nil. It shut him up almost immediately.

The following week I was on my way to central London. It was quite a long walk to Kidbrooke Railway Station and I'd pin-pointed just where Fetter Lane was. A bus ride from Charing Cross Station, along the Strand into Fleet Street. Because of the war, it was the first time I had ever been on a train to anywhere. Thanks to the Bank of Mum, I travelled third class in a carriage with minimal comfort. Wooden seats with no cushion or covering of any kind. And, would you believe, there were "Ladies Only" compartments too. It was a journey I was committed to making six days a week for the next four years. Then it would be the final year before National Service was to be disbanded, the year I would be ordered to serve my King and Country. The year I was enlisted in the Royal Air Force, I had left home early and arrived at the *Sunday Pictorial* with almost an hour to spare. There were two uniformed male receptionists kept continually busy with endless ringing phones, visitors who kept coming and going, messengers and deliveries that never ceased. It was exactly as I had imagined a busy newspaper's offices should be. And glory be, in no time at all I would be a junior member of this exciting new way of life. Not bad at all, I thought, for the boy from a south east London council estate.

Before ten minutes of my first-ever job interview had passed, all beliefs I held about a journalistic career were cruelly shattered. Certainly where the *Sunday Pictorial* and other national newspapers were concerned. So said the fifty-something grey-haired female harbinger of gloom sitting opposite me. She was head of human resources and had my letter in front of her. She went to great lengths to explain that nobody came to this newspaper to be trained as a journalist. They already were journalists of merit. Men who had trained on umpteen local papers before being invited into the world of daily and weekly Fleet Street newspapers. She went on to explain what I should do next. Take my chance that I would be experienced enough having served the necessary local-press apprenticeship. Plus luck and loads of it. And providing there was a need for an experienced all-rounder or a specialist writer who fitted the specification. Then, and only then, would I be taken on board.

She could see the disappointment on my face and her voice softened. "So you can see what you have to do. It won't be easy as you now know. So, what do you think?"

When I finally spoke it was to ask her why she

had not written to tell me. Her answer came as a great surprise. "I found your letter interesting and wanted to meet you. There is a vacancy that I thought you might like, available at the end of the month. Now I've met you I know you can fill it." She went on to say that she had spoken to Nick Carter who ran her department. "He'd like to see you before you leave. If he likes you, Frank, the job's yours. Shall we go see him?"

As I followed Mrs Pitman to the lift, my mind was in turmoil. By the time we reached Mr Carter's office, I decided if I liked him and was offered the position, I'd take it. Whatever it was. And I did. Long before Nick had finished outlining my duties as the newest tape room boy to join the powerful ranks of the *Sunday Pictorial*, I must admit to having had reservations. The strongest of which was the undeniable fact that a tape room employee differed little from the go-for my step-father laid at my door. If he ever found out, I'd have to leave home to escape the incessant rhetoric coming my way. Or hand in my notice immediately. So I told him I was to work with the picture desk, assisting the photographers on photo shoots when needed. Which is precisely what happened. In fact, as a tape room boy, it was the most exciting, interesting and, in many aspects, absorbing employment I ever had. Time and again I was called upon to perform duties that tested my capabilities to the full, and then some. I can honestly say there were rarely two days alike. And I loved it. Working for a big-circulation popular daily and weekly newspaper group was like growing up in the fast lane. From day one I was the envy of my peers.

In all, there were four tape room boys under Nick Carter's control. He was informed of the needs of the moment and detailed one of us accordingly. The needs were wide and varied: from food from the canteen, collecting packages and typed copy from rail stations or features writers' homes, purchasing cigarettes and different items from Fleet Street shops. These comprised the majority of jobs we did. I always showed willing, as most were accompanied by tips from whoever ordered the items. I soon got to know who tipped the most, the least and not at all. The generous and the tight-wads. This was important, as my wage was £1.50 weekly which I shared equally with my mother. Then there was the daily morning trip to the upstairs canteen which I fought hard to make my own.

When my funds were running low, for a small consideration I would persuade whoever's turn it was to let me do the canteen run for them. Newspapermen's consumption of tea, coffee and confectionery was prodigious. As most were reluctant to venture the three floors to the canteen, they had little idea of actual prices. But I did. Right down to the last sausage roll. So, depending on how broke I was, I fibbed a little – sometimes more than a little. But never more than twenty five percent. I had long since convinced myself what I did was opportunistic deceit, rather than dishonest money manipulation. I had also spent more than a little time winning the motherly affection and trust of Peggy, the cashier. I would tell her precisely the edible items I had in the large box, covered by a tea towel emphasising my concern with hygiene. It was always a new, clean tea towel. Something which I considered well worth the small cost outlay. For never once did Peggy ask me to remove it, enabling her to check what lay beneath. Did I have a conscience? No, not really. They could afford the few pence I added to each item purchased. It was my commission for services rendered. After all, I carried out the wishes of the sports, art and news desk occupants to the last letter. Often doing things not in my job specification. So, I figured the buggers I was buying for should pay a little extra. I was simply collecting my due reward for extra services rendered.

In all, the mix of people I worked with and for were exceptional. There were some who made certain I was, and remained, a tape room boy. I left those to my colleagues whenever I could. I spent most of my time close to the needs of the picture and sports desk personnel. Peter Thompson was the senior football correspondent, who took a great shine to me. The first time we met, he told everybody I was the spitting image of Jimmy Dickinson, the Portsmouth football club captain and England international. I was flattered, as from that moment on, he forever called me Jimmy. When I thought the time was right, I told him I had a burning ambition to become a sports reporter, after which he would often sit and tell me how he got started, reporting local matches for the local press until he got his break with the *Sunday Pic* several years back. He suggested I cover local lower-league football matches and submit them to him to read. Later, he added local boxing matches, which were his second sporting love.

He was a great help and encouraged me no end. One day, he told me that once I had completed my National Service, he would introduce me to people who could be useful in helping me achieve my ambition. That is if it was still my ambition once demobbed. I told him I had no doubts it would be, but that a two-year break with the RAF was never going to be helpful. As indeed it wasn't. By strange coincidence, on the bill of a local boxing match at Eltham Baths, the Cooper twins were appearing. They were both heavyweights and both won their fights. Jim, by the narrowest of points, Henry, by stopping his opponent in the third of a six-round fight. Having watched both fights, I felt then that Henry would go far but not so Jim. He didn't, and quit boxing by the year's end. Soon after, a lady joined my mum working in the Dover Patrol pub. It was the Cooper's mother and she and my mum became firm friends.

SEVEN

S mile please, you're on camera.

There were six permanent men manning the picture desk and I made absolutely certain I was liked by each and every one, before I was legally kidnapped by the Royal Air Force to undertake National Service. It paid handsome dividends as you will see. Jack Crawshaw was the pictures editor, responsible for the final selection of every non-sports picture which appeared in each week's issue. Jack smoked at least fifty cigarettes daily. He smoked Goldflake and I was sent out at least once a day to replenish his supply. He coughed incessantly and vowed daily to give it up but never did whilst I was there. His assistant art editor was Ben Jones, ex-Navy. Probably in his early thirties, he publicly encouraged Jack's nicotine intake, openly telling him he was after his job. What's more, Jack knew it, but they made a brilliant working team and were really Mickey-taking best friends.

As we were a Sunday paper we all worked Saturdays. My working day started at nine o'clock and I rarely left for home before six. A long, very busy and exciting day for a young boy involved in putting a leading national newspaper to bed. From the earliest northern edition to the final fifth London and southern editions. It amused me when my fellow train passengers tried hard to read my copy of the *Pic*, which I always took home with me. Most not believing I had tomorrow's paper today. Then, when reading the date, wondered how and where I got it. I waited to be asked and then I told them

When I arrived at work on this particular Saturday, Ben's phone was ringing non-stop. As I picked it up, I could hear an unknown voice screaming, "Ben, pick up this fucking phone! Ben, where the fucking hell are you?" It turned out to be our West Country correspondent and he sounded frantic. There was serious flooding and loss of life in Lynton and Lynmouth, Devon. The whole area was now cut off and no rescue services could get through to those trapped. To show the full extent of the flooding, he said we needed to get a photographer airborne. Now. I told him I was already dialling Ben Jones.

When Ben answered the phone, he sounded half asleep. When I finished telling him what was happening in the West Country, he was mid-way through frantically dressing. Now in a panic, he told me to ring

Mortons Air Service in Croydon. Tell them to prepare our usual aircraft and put our usual pilot on standby. He would ring photographer Bill Turner who lived nearest to the airport and tell him there was an aircraft awaiting his arrival and what was happening in Devon. Now a photographer was on his way. So was Ben. True to his word, he arrived soon after and within seconds he had taken command of the situation. It had happened within forty-five minutes of my arrival in the office. Before Jack Crawshaw arrived, we had everything under control. I quietly thought, "Ben Jones, you owe me one." And to give him his due, thereafter he organised that most of the future quality jobs had my name on them without raising suspicion of favouritism. Although I suspect he had tipped off my immediate boss, Nick Carter. A great bloke to have in your corner, as he was in mine. Let me give you a for instance.

The *Pic* had four resident photographers on their payroll. Of the four, I believe Percy Bosher was the most imaginative. Frankie Laine, the famous American country and western singer, was playing the London Palladium. On the same show was Nancy Crompton, allegedly the fastest pirouette dancer in the world. Percy had the bright idea of stringing lots of different coloured fairy lights all over her slim, young body And Nancy loved the idea. So did Frankie Laine's management, as it would be additional cost-free mid-show publicity. The bonus for the *Pic*. A pretty young dancer, totally encapsulated by circles of mixed spinning coloured-lights. Brilliant photography and another photo exclusive to the *Pic*. My bonus was assisting Percy light the shoot, killing unwanted shadows. The pleasure of running my hands over an attractive, young "body beautiful" whilst stringing the lights in place. She was a true artist, but sadly one whom I was destined never to see again. Being a rather randy young bugger, on this occasion, meeting Frankie Laine was an also ran. But not for long. It was a most enjoyable morning, except for one thing. I was warned to press my bum hard against anything solid, because if I didn't I would be groped by the show's drag queen. He kept appearing on stage and would have been a pain in the arse. Mine if I let him.

Some months before I joined the *Pic*, Ben had set up an arrangement with the Rank Film Organisation. Whenever they discovered a potential young film starlet, Chris Simpson, Rank's man responsible for introducing the said starlets to the great British public, contacted Ben. By appointment, Chris would bring them to Geraldine House for Ben to decide whether they met with his and Jack's approval. If yes, it was agreed, there and then, that she would adorn the pages of probably the best-selling national Sunday newspaper of the fifties. Unless sick or on holiday, Ben having told me in advance what and where the shoot was, mine were the chosen pair of helping hands delegated. My Lynton and Lynmouth bonus was paying handsome dividends.

Do you know any other teenage boy who not only met the lovely Mai Zetterling, but later had the exciting pleasure of covering this truly beautiful Swedish Rank Film starlet in flowers? When Chris brought her to the picture desk, she totally won the lust of both Ben and me. Plus, Jack's full admiration for this delightfully sexy, blonde Swedish nymph. As for me, I was somewhere between the two. But the best was yet to come. Percy Bosher was the specialist glamour picture taker. As it was early spring, he decided St James's Park was the ideal location. Plus, it was close to where Mai lived. But, as unreliable as ever, the weather decided otherwise and, whilst loading the photographic kit and floodlights into Percy's car, the heavens opened. This unexpected disaster called for an immediate plan B. Percy had one. He would drive to Mai's flat and explain that because of the heavy rain, the photo shoot would take place right there in Mai's apartment.

And so it did. But not before Percy had thrust white five-pound notes in my hand and told me to grab a taxi, which I did, and spend all of the money on daffodils, which I did. When the cabbie and I unloaded them in Mai's flat, Percy was already there, busy setting up his camera, lights and other props used to help create the look of spring. Whilst it wasn't St James's Park, critically strewn oodles of daffs soon converted the lounge of Mai's flat into the next best thing. All that was missing was our Swedish starlet. Then, she appeared, wearing the tiniest of yellow bikinis you ever did see. Percy remained impassive as she arranged her divine body on the flower-covered rug. Not so much me. My hands were trembling as I strategically placed the daffodils upon her prone body. She giggled, then winked at me as I stepped back from my delightful chore. Every time she changed position I rearranged her floral decor. And each time more of her desirable curves were displayed, I fell hopelessly in love. Remaining so to this very day. Having starred in films for Rank, Mai eventually returned to Sweden, where she continued working in films.

Other Rank starlets came and went. And whenever the selected photographer needed a helping hand, guess who was seconded to the shoot. I touched the flesh of Diana Dors, Susan Shaw and Simone Silva amongst others. Also, one voluptuous young lady by name of Sandra Dorne, who dressed as a bus conductress. Why, I will never know, as the ill-fitting uniform left bunches of pubic hair on show either side of the uniform's very skimpy short pants. It was used in the *Pic*, but extremely heavily retouched I would add. Whilst the helping hands, mine, could not stop trembling. Nor could I control the stirring in my loins, encouraged as I was by each and every curvy pose, some of which bordered on pornographic. Going back to Mai Zetterling for a moment, I never saw her again, except for appearances in Rank films. Eventually she returned to Sweden and became one of that country's foremost film directors.

I truly enjoyed working with all of the *Pictorial*'s various groups. But most of all Ben Jones and the picture desk crew, where rarely, if ever, were two days' activities the same. It was 1952 and in September I would depart. For two years I was to become a member of the Royal Air Force. Not voluntarily, I would add, but as a national serviceman. Like most blokes of my age, we thought conscription a complete waste of time. Especially as it was abandoned the year after I was 'captured'. If both the picture and sports desks were intent on giving me a good farewell in September, what they actually did was formidable.

It was mid-February 1952 and I was giving Jack Crawshaw his change along with his twenty Gold Flake. "Ever been to the Grand National, Frank?" he asked. I told him I hadn't and was never likely to. But I had seen it on the cinema newsreels. "Well," said Jack, "you've worked hard for us and the sports lads. So this year we've decided you are going to Aintree. It's our way of saying thanks, knowing we can rely on you." Not only was I gobsmacked, but also delighted with the compliments given. When I arrived home, I made certain that this useless go-for informed his step-father of his Grand National good news. Naturally embellished with enviable porkies.

I thought of nothing else on the train journey home. I couldn't wait to tell my mother, which I did no sooner than I walked through the door. She was most pleased and the next day would tell all her friends and neighbours, of my very important role in the coming Grand National. I then took great pleasure in confronting my step-father, giving him full details of what I would be doing as an important member of a national newspaper team. Whilst he would still be pedalling around the streets emptying gas metres. He didn't like it one little bit. I loved it all. Especially the embellishments.

The forthcoming 1952 Grand National had worldwide recognition. Our start to finish coverage meeting, which I was asked to attend, was meticulous. Planned with almost military precision, I quickly realised how much depended on me getting it right. I was to accompany photographer Malcolm McNeil to the first jump on the inside of the course. He would be using a wide-angle plate camera and I was to hold spare plates, enabling Mac to capture the expected carnage from the largest ever field assembled at Aintree. I was then to rush the photographic plate efforts of Mac's picture-taking, with all speed, to the course hotel. There, in the hotel basement, the *Pic* production team would be waiting to wire the pictures back to Geraldine House. Once received, they would be included in the first of the five printed editions of the *Pic*. I would then race back to the finishing post and collect film taken by all the other *Pic* photographers elsewhere on the course, including pictures of the winner and other finishers of the race. The last photograph needed was of the winner in the unsaddling enclosure, together with the owners, winning jockey and trainer. Once I had everything, I would race to the car waiting to deliver me to the nearby airfield. There, a private aircraft would be waiting to fly me to Morton Air Services in Croydon. Finally, I would jump in another car to whisk me to the *Sunday Pictorial* and deliver the last of the pictures taken to the picture desk. Result. Mission accomplished. Messenger knackered.

April 4th. Departure day had arrived. The combined *Pic* team converged on Aintree en masse. Journalists, photographers and production team complete with the latest photo-wiring kit. The air of anticipation was present. Each *Pic* team member was well-rehearsed in the part he would play and confident that our published end report, Grand National news and picture coverage would not be surpassed. And it wasn't. I travelled by train to Liverpool and met with rest of the team at our comfortable overnight hotel. I had my own room for which I was grateful, as it was the first hotel I had ever stayed in. We gathered for dinner, which included something for everyone, vegetarians included. After dinner, we repaired to the bar. I went too, but, because of my tender years, I was not (by law) allowed alcoholic beverages. So I sat and listened to some truly amazing stories concerning the many previous sporting events they had photographically covered. It was then I realised just how privileged I was.

I sat next to Malcolm at breakfast and I asked if we could run through when, where and what I would be doing once the race began. He corrected me when I faltered, but, by the time we were in the car heading for Aintree, I knew my routine backwards. Neither

Malcolm nor I could be blamed for the false start caused by one horse charging the starting tape. Had it ever happened before in the 150-year history of the race? The general opinion of the knowledgeable group of press and emergency staff assembled at the first jump was no. Whatever the correct answer, the start was delayed by ten minutes. We had been there for an hour already and we were all soaked by a continuous light drizzle, puddles forming at our feet. The mood was black. The weather foul. The mist thickening by the moment. Looking back towards the start, you could see less than 150 yards. You could hear the horses, excitedly awaiting the off. Also those jockeys who weren't quite ready to go. The noise from the crowded stand, urging the starter to get the race started. Peering into the mist, all this we could hear, but none of it could we see.

Malcolm had his plate camera dry under his jacket and I had three spare plates under mine. Then I heard it. A mighty roar from the crowd, instantly followed by the noise of the jockeys straining to get the 1952 Grand National underway. Then they were off. I heard all of this but saw nothing. Suddenly there was a magnificent line of colour exploding out of the mist. Stretching the whole width of the Grand National course. More than forty charging horses, line abreast, thundering toward the first obstacle. A sight I will never forget. Man and beast soaring into Aintree's mist-shrouded afternoon. Crashing through the hawthorn-topped first jump. Up and over, down and out. The mist descending once again as the last of the racing horses galloped away, some now without their man in the saddle. Leaving behind a scene of carnage: horses struggling to their feet, others lying still, not moving. Flanks quivering. Softly neighing as if asking for help. Riders lying still beside their mounts, incapable of giving help as they needed it themselves. I was seventeen and I saw it all. I stood transfixed. It wasn't sport, it was mayhem.

I saw everything but heard nothing. Not even Malcom screaming, "Give me the fucking plates", as he made a wild grab for the three plates sheltering under my jacket. I was shocked into action as Mac tore the first from my hand. He rapidly ran back to the terrible scene of injured horses and riders lying in front of him. He wanted a damning picture of a race many wanted banned. He got three.

With all four plates used and safely under my jacket, I was on my way to the course hotel. I arrived breathless and handed over my precious cargo. In a flash, the production team were preparing the plates for wiring to their colleagues in Geraldine House. My job done, I was on my way back to the unsaddling enclosure. When I arrived, Mac was already there and I apologised profusely for how I had reacted. He was none too happy at my behaviour but was pleased with the shots he had got. He believed the fallers at the first jump were the largest number of casualties ever. There were also fallers at the seventh fence and only ten horses officially finished the race. The winner was Teal, trained by Aintree-specialist Neville Crump. Rumours had it he would enter Teal again in 1953, but sadly it never happened. Teal would wrench his gut while racing at Cheltenham, he never raced again.

I could not believe the sight that greeted me when I returned to the unsaddling enclosure. A close look at the horses revealed their legs, especially their withers, were savagely torn and bleeding. For some time, public opinion had been pleading with the Aintree course owner, Mrs Topham, to lower the jumps by at least six inches and to stop topping them with hawthorn, an unforgiving hedge plant whose sharp thorns caused such horrific injuries. It was sixty-seven years ago, but this time she listened and agreed. I waited until all ceremonies ended, collected all the undeveloped film and found the car and climbed in. Then we were off to the small Aintree airport. It took me a little while to find my Morton Services aircraft. Longer to find the pilot, who was happily swapping stories with other pilots, who were also awaiting their human cargo, in the bar. Being Grand National day, it was one of, if not the busiest day of the racing calendar. Having been cleared for take-off, we were up, up and away. Back to Croydon where the Rolls-Royce and chauffeur for the *Mirror/Pictorial* group chairman awaited my arrival. When Ben Jones first told me of the Aintree arrangements as they affected me, I cheekily asked if he could get the chauffeur to wear his peaked hat. He actually went one better and wore the full bloody livery. Cap that if you can. Me, a seventeen-year-old council house kid from south east London, a privileged VIP at the greatest horse race in the world, being flown home in a private aeroplane and collected by a liveried chauffeur in a Rolls Royce. A story I loved to tell. One most people found it hard to believe, but I knew differently because I was there from beginning to end. My final six months before freedom disappeared passed all too quickly, but I'm convinced those I worked with made sure I enjoyed every day. Especially Peter Thomson. He not only encouraged me to continue covering various sporting events, but also read the reports I submitted. By the time September arrived, I was convinced that once I had completed my two years National Service, I would be offered a job on the *Sunday Pictorial*'s sports desk. Before I left, Ben Jones told me the crew at the picture desk had arranged a week's holiday at Butlin's holiday camp in Skegness. It was a lovely gesture. One which I considered had wiped Ben's Lynton and Lynmouth slate clean.

EIGHT

For Queen and Country.

For the very first time in my young life, as I shut the front door to 30 Birdbrook Road, I felt lonely. And hungover from the previous night's long and pint-packed farewell. I had no idea how long it would be before I walked through my front door again, nor what was likely to happen between now and then. I'd made up my mind it wasn't going to be pleasant. The only advice given by my stepbrother, who had finished his National Service four years previously, was that the eight weeks square-bashing at Wilmslow, where I was heading, were hideous. Do everything the drill corporals tell you. You'll hate it, but they'll hate you more. Get stuck in and time will fly. Keep your nose clean for eight weeks and you're a winner, upset the bastards and you'll be a goner. A definite loser. One who won't realise just how difficult life will become. I dwelt on these pearls of wisdom while I was standing on the station platform waiting for the Warrington train to arrive. What Warrington was like I had no idea – I had never travelled further north than Arsenal Football Club – but I was soon to find out. My thoughts firmly fixed on tomorrow, I'd failed to notice there were quite a number of passengers now awaiting the arrival of the train. I immediately knew who the two young guys closest to me were. They had National Service written all over them, but, to make sure, I walked over and asked. Introductions were made just as the train arrived. Norman "Call me Bunny" Whelan and Derek Finch. By the time we pulled away, we had been joined by three others: Albert Hollis, Chris Baker and Gerry Conrad.

None of us knew each other, but each of us shared the same air of nervous expectancy. We were all too soon to reluctantly embark upon a new life. Exchanging Civvy Street for two years in the Royal Air Force. Each of us different, yet each one of us sharing the same outward signs of bravado, tinged with nervous apprehension. The tough exterior. False laughter at every utterance. Determined to kick discipline into touch. Beat the system. Do your own thing, not theirs. Bonk WRAFs (they were all gagging for it, weren't they?) Full of misgivings and fearful of what lay ahead, but, above all else, determined to survive.

The first fifteen minutes of our journey into the unknown revealed why Whelan was called Bunny.

He just never stopped "rabbiting". The rest of us were regaled with the Whelan family history all the way back to the battle of Hastings. Somewhere along the way, we were able to extract that Bunny worked on a market stall in Smithfield. He hailed from Shepherds Bush and, for his sins, supported Queens Park Rangers FC. He had a girlfriend, who told him as he said goodbye she was up the duff. His final comment was, "What the fuck should I do? Her Dad will fucking kill me." I couldn't resist it and told him to get off the train, wherever he could, and join the Foreign Legion.

By this time we were now engaged in playing no money cards, which gave me the chance to form mental pictures of the others. Derek Finch wasn't difficult. The first clue was his soft, well-manicured hands, then his ability to quickly add up points won in each card game played. He was, as I expected, a number cruncher who worked for Midland Bank. He hated it, as he admitted later. Roy Baker wasn't difficult either. Slightly rotund, pink cheeks, eyes like bruised fruit, cakes and pastries eaten virtually non-stop. Food loomed large in Roy's (or Doughy's, as he became known) life. As well it should when he told us his parents owned a small south London bakery in New Cross. Albert Hollis was the mystery. A little over six foot tall, bone-rattling skinny, his civvies just hung on him. He looked every inch an undertakers assistant. In fact, that's what I honestly believed him to be. I couldn't have been so wrong as Hollis revealed he earned good money, as a part-time kiddies entertainer.

When he wasn't doing that, he was unloading cargo in Tilbury Dock. And so to Gerry Conrad. The last and easiest of the London sixsome. His family were extremely wealthy, allowing Gerry to continue his education until call-up. He was a lucky sod.

So there we were. Six of us travelling north at Her Majesty's request. All expenses paid. Our destination: RAF Wilmslow, where we were to undergo our basic training. Square-bashing, as my step-brother had informed me. Eight long tortuous weeks at the mercy of corporal drill instructors, devoid of all humanity once their umbilical cords had been severed. Each team determined to have the best squad of raw recruits at the end of training. Not one of them caring how this would be achieved, nor how many of us would live to tell the tale. Warrington was the next stop where we would change trains for RAF Wilmslow. Or so we thought.

Bunny kept wanting to play cards for money and whinged incessantly when the rest of us said no. We all agreed to smoke our own cigarettes, as money would be very short from now on. This I knew. My step-brother told me, it was pre-decimalisation and sterling was the currency. I then told them our wage was to be a weekly sum of twenty-one shillings. "Fuck me." said Bunny. "I spend that and more every night in the fucking pub." Where we sat in the carriage was now ankle-deep in litter of every description. Cigarette ends and empty packets, sweet wrappings, drink cartons, cans and cake papers. We told the guard, when he came to check our travel warrants, not to worry – we would pick it all up. About twenty minutes out from Warrington, he came back and stood over us while we did. Then the train started to slow as it eased its way into Warrington Station. We each collected our baggage and prepared to alight. Being Bunny, he just had to have the last word. As he opened the carriage door, he said in a very loud voice, "What's that fucking pong?"

For once, Bunny was not exaggerating. The stench of carbolic soap was overpowering. Breathe deeply and you wretched. breathe normally and you gagged. My step-brother had never warned me about the Warrington stench, nor what happened next. As if by magic, the platform was suddenly full of uniformed corporals. Uniforms immaculately pressed. Cap badges, buttons and boots gleaming in the late-afternoon sun. Slashed hat peaks just touching the bridge of every corporal's nose. They came wreathed in discipline, enshrined in centuries of military bullshit, accompanied by one warrant officer. Each intent on terrorising the group of petrified new arrivals spread along the platform. It worked a treat as his henchmen came amongst us. He bellowed his first command, "Get your fucking things together and form up in the car park. At the double." This the corporals echoed like parrots, word for word, pushing and shoving us through the open station doors. Awaiting us were three Bedford three-tonners. Again the warrant officer appeared, issuing his second command, "You lot and your things. On the fucking trucks. At the double." This was the corporals' cue to get physically involved and the air became full of multi-accented, bellowed profanities. Most of which I knew, but the very lewd ones I didn't. I had anticipated why the trucks were there. So I was one of the first on board the nearest vehicle, not one of the slow to act. I witnessed their arses and bags being kicked, backs shoved, heads slapped. A few of the corporals turned out to be our drill instructors. The one who seemed to be the most violent, in word and deed, was Scottish. He was really getting off on our mass humiliation. And somehow I knew I would be in his squad. And I was. As the trucks pulled away, packed full of terrified and mystified raw recruits, I heard a low, petrified voice mutter, "I thought the fucking Gestapo were all fucking dead." You're right, it was Bunny. My silent thoughts were, "Bunny, my son, you don't know the half of it." Trouble was, nor did I.

We clung to each other as our Bedford did its level best to be the first to reach RAF Wilmslow. Whatever conversation took place was barely audible. Bunny the Buffoon lit a cigarette, even though no smoking warning notices were everywhere you looked. Before he could take a single puff, a voice from nowhere screamed, "Put that fucking fag out or I'll stuff it down your fucking throat!" It was a voice we came to despise. It was Corporal Gerry Hodgson. And he was all ours for the next eight weeks.

NINE

No sooner did the Wilmslow camp gates swing open and the Bedfords lurch to a halt than all hell broke loose. What looked like a squad of demented uniformed air force personnel boarded all three trucks. Shouting, shoving, snarling, swearing. They were amongst us in a flash. All resistance and would-be bravado vanished. Baggage and bodies rained down to the accompanying shouts of, "Out, out, out you 'orrible bastards! Off this fucking truck at the double!" Panic ensued and confusion took over. The noise was deafening. They wanted control and they had it as soon as the shouting began. We were swiftly bullied into lines and marched away to the centre of the parade ground. There we waited. Fearful of the unknown, but still we waited. Cowed, weary and getting hungrier by the frightening minute. Standing stiffly to attention. Not speaking.

Some, like me, in need of urinating. Waiting for what? We had been waiting a long time, so I figured it was someone or something important.

I guess the group captain commanding RAF Wilmslow wasn't just important. He was looked upon by the RAF personnel present as a deity. Sadly, my bladder did not share the same respect and without warning I part peed my pants. I wasn't embarrassed. Just bloody angry, bloody hungry and decidedly uncomfortable. He welcomed us, one and all – the dry and the comfortable, the wet and the angry – then proceeded to tell us why we were there, what to expect while we were there, what to do while we were there, what not to do while we were there, how to survive while we were there and how long we could expect to be there. He departed leaving us this message, "For the next eight weeks it will seem like hell on earth, gentlemen. That's because it will be. But at the end you'll be a credit to Her Majesty's Royal Air Force. If not, you'll be our guest for as long as it takes." Then he was gone.

Now it was the turn of the non-commissioned officers to take control. They did with a vengeance. Namely corporals, working in teams of three. We were bullied into three flights and marched, at the double, to the Nissen huts on the far side of the parade ground. Three flights of thirty-two conscripts per hut. Once inside, we were told to choose and stand by a bed, any bed. We did so, at the double. The names of our tormentors were then made known to us. Each was a drill instructor in his own right. Their seniority decided by experience.

We all knew the one who introduced himself first. It was the foul-mouthed, foul-tempered, florid-faced Corporal Gerry Hodgson. I stood just a few feet from him and his unwashed body odour was unmistakable. I was close enough to look directly into his eyes; they were dead, they were sunken. A lifeless colour of excremental brown rather like solidified diarrhoea. From that moment on, I named him Turd Eyes. A name immediately adopted by every member of A Flight. It probably stayed with him long after I left RAF Wilmslow for my new posting. I rather hoped so. It suited him to a tee.

His opening remarks, almost undecipherable because of his heavy Scottish accent, said it all as far as I was concerned. "My name is Hodgson. Corporal Hodgson. That's how you will address me. I am your fucking worst fucking nightmare. The one you've just heard about from the group captain." He then named his two colleagues, corporals Leith and Wilkins. He continued for the next twenty minutes or so, telling us what was going to happen in the coming eight weeks. What we heard struck the fear of God into all of us. We were then told to form up in ranks of three and told we were being taken to the airmen's mess to eat. We were told to unpack our belongings and leave them tidily on our beds. To my dismay, there were no mattresses, just three straw-filled "biscuits" laid end-to-end on the bedsprings. They had no give and looked as worn and uncomfortable as they proved to be. Hodgson's two colleagues remained behind while he decided to drill us in the art of marching. For close to an hour we were marched back and forth on the parade ground – turning left, then right, turning about, halting. Dressing, first right, then left. Profanely berated for the myriad of mistakes new recruits were entitled to make.

Tired, exhausted, beaten and bemused, the torture ended as dusk gathered. We were finally dismissed and allowed to enter the mess to savour our first taste of RAF cuisine. We were hungry enough to have eaten each other – pity the poor bugger who was served Turd Eyes. In truth, whether or not acute hunger had affected our taste buds, it wasn't at all bad. And there was a reasonable amount per recruit. Now replete, by Turd Eyes returned and we were marched directly back to our Nissen hut. And, thank God, it was too dark to have to repeat our marching drill. But none of us could have predicted what awaited us when we re-entered our home for the next eight weeks.

No sooner dismissed, Bunny Whelan was first through the Nissen door, "Fucking hell! Look at the fucking mess." Personal belongings littered every inch of the highly polished floor, topped by every thin, straw-filled bed biscuit. Every bed-space had been blitzed. Hodgson's sidekicks were the villains. It would take till midnight, sorting through the mess and reclaiming what belonged to whom. Not one of us heard Turd Eyes enter: "What the fucking hell do you think we gave you each a tin locker for? That's where your fucking belongings should be. Not on the fucking floor." These were the first words he uttered, grinning like a Cheshire cat. "I want every fucking thing in its proper place by lights out at ten o'clock." We worked tirelessly, not daring to get undressed for bed, awaiting the second coming of Turd Eyes. He finally returned from the non-commissioned officers' mess, drunk as a skunk, stumbling and mumbling into his quarters. Never to re-emerge again that night.

Being after midnight, as one man, we decided he had no right to deprive us of sleep. So we decided to get undressed, make our wafer-thin biscuits into mattresses and go to bed. Absolutely exhausted, defeated. Wondering just what tomorrow would bring. This being our first night in the RAF, the thin, straw-filled biscuits, lumpy pillows and coarse blankets were not conducive to sleeping, as most of us discovered. The events of the day held sleep at arm's length. I lay there, vowing not to let Turd Eyes get the better of me. I would get through this nightmare. It was, after all, only eight weeks. Not eight months. Keep your head down, nose clean, do everything asked of you and it would soon pass. Incur the wrath of Turd Eyes at your peril.

How he did it, only the good Lord knows. In partnership with nature, he rose with dawn. The first any of us knew was a screamed, "Hands off cocks, on with socks!" accompanied by Turd Eyes beating his swagger-stick against our metal lockers. Those of us whose feet were slow to grace the polished floor were unceremoniously dumped from their beds by Lieth and Wilkins. Then, in only our underpants, we were formed up outside and doubled to the latrines. There, all thirty-two of us were ordered to, "Hurry up and shit, shave and fucking shampoo", before being doubled back to our billet. Given the ten minutes to do as ordered, you would think it was time enough, but when there were only twenty showers, hand basins, mirrors and thunder-box cubicles available to thirty-two half-asleep new recruits, I can assure you, it wasn't.

Once back, the daily ritual began. A close inspection by the three Drill Instructors. Shaving cuts and nicks classified as abusing your person. Those so afflicted were charged with causing self-inflicted wounds in order to miss morning parade – a serious violation of Queen's regulations. But then, every small thing they searched long and hard for met with the same fate. Once satisfied enough charges had been recorded, we were told to don the working RAF uniform before being doubled to the airmen's mess for breakfast. Once finished, we were marched back to our billet for our first morning kit inspection. Having been shown how to prepare our kit for inspection, the special layout and presentation format was quickly demonstrated. You commenced with your mattress biscuits placed on top of each other. Your blankets followed, perfectly squared to exact measurements and serving as a platform for the rest of the kit required. This had a special layout format and position. It was sacrosanct, with each item being spotlessly clean and highly polished. All now in special inspection order. Once the inspection began, you stood stiffly to attention, eyes front. Being our first ever kit inspection, you would expect mistakes to occur and they did. But not to the extent the inspecting warrant officer should criticise every airmen's kit. Before he finally left, not one of our honest attempts was left standing. Some, often most, were swept contemptuously to the floor. Charges followed in droves for just about everything laid out and not one of us escaped. All charges were recorded by the accompanying drill instructors and very little notice was given of when the next inspection would be. Virtually no time at all to meet each inspection's demands. But we coped – well, most of us did – and some even finished with time to spare and were able to help those in trouble. In the beginning, the "fizzers" (charges) came thick and fast. So much so, the officers responsible for listening to charges and issuing suitable punishments ran out of ideas. During this period, my admonishments included scraping the long-dried, white urine stains off the men's stand-up iron latrines with a razor blade, emptying dirty water from the parade ground puddles and refilling them with clean water and painting the top layers of coal white in the camp's many coal bunkers This, I was told, was at the request of the Air Officer Commanding Second Tactical Air Force when he last visited RAF Sylt. He said they would look smart with white tops. What an absolute load of cobblers. I was tempted to write to him, in a moment of madness, suggesting I cut the grass in front of the officers' mess with nail scissors, or a knife and fork. Hurriedly dismissed, for fear it might be taken seriously.

TEN

You will have gathered by now just how life for the would-be airmen of A Flight was totally unlike anything experienced on Civvy Street. For instance, which one of us would have gone to an abattoir for a haircut. Once behind the gates of RAF Wilmslow, it was obligatory. You were marched, en masse, to a large hanger where recruits with sheep-shearing experience were gathered. Each was given a pair of scissors and electric clippers, then let loose amongst unsuspecting Flight A conscripts. Their orders were to cut each recruit's hair in three minutes flat. The result, as near as dammit, a bald airman. Whatever your hairstyle before your three minutes arrived, it was very soon looking up at you from the floor. Styles mattered not, all met the same fate. You didn't ask. You didn't dare. The order of the day. Every day, in fact. Short back and sides, the shorter the better. Honed by years of inexperience. It was sacrosanct. The first and last time I've seen grown men cry as their three minute ordeal ended.

Apart from Sundays, "Hands off cocks, on with socks" became your regular waking dawn chorus. At the speed of light, you climbed into your baggy RAF drawers, collected your toiletries and formed up outside your billet. Once inside the toilet block you fought for your place in front of a mirror. Toilet needs satisfied, back to billets. Dress. Collect your mug and eating irons and march to the Airmen's Mess. Choose and consume breakfast. March back to billet and lay out kit for inspection. Inspection over, prepare for morning parade. Before parade dismissal, you were informed of that day's activities. The next two hours spent marching drill (referred to as square-bashing) with and without your Enfield 303 rifle for pass-out parade rehearsal. Dismissed for a one-hour lunch. Afternoons were spent on lectures and stripping down and rebuilding Bren guns. Then to the rifle range to practice getting used to firing your Enfield 303. The one time the hated Turd Eyes went absent. Why? We used live ammunition, need I say more. Occasionally and without warning, we were told to don our full packs as we were off for a run through the Pennines. The distances were gradually increased and the final distance was five miles. Quite a few of us finished the last half-mile walking. Others had to be collected and were charged with disobeying orders. Almost without exception, the 'jankers' (punishment) was dreaded cook-house fatigues. This entailed unlocking the airmen's mess at 5 a.m. As you switched on the lights, the whole of the large dining-room floor was on the move. Cockroaches. Literally hundreds of the nasty little buggers disturbed by the light, and running for their lives. Except those crunching under your feet. When the last had disappeared, you moved amongst the fifty or so dining tables, each with large metal bowls of jam or marmalade at each end that were inches deep with cockroaches, which you proceeded to scrape off the top with large wooden spoons. Once cleansed, you washed the revolting sticky mess from the spoons down the kitchen sinks and waited for the cooks (no way could you possibly mistake them for chefs) to arrive. Your job then was to assist them in the preparation of breakfast for the whole camp. This you did, but having battled with the huge army of cockroaches earlier, you had little appetite left.

Each day was fully programmed – Turd Eyes made certain of that. By the time we signalled we were ready to eat at the end of the day, Corporals Lieth and Wilkins were happy to agree. But not Turd Eyes. Having returned to our billet, he would order us back onto the parade ground. What we then did depended on the mood he was in. His favourite was performing rifle drill whilst marching continuously until he, not us, was ready to eat. This quite often meant that, in our mess, the most appetising meals had long since been devoured. Which left you with two choices: either eat what remained or starve. Once back in the billet, there was little time left to repair the day's ravages to our kit layout before lights out. Result. More charges and more jankers on tomorrow's parade.

There was no let-up in our daily routines. We knew there wouldn't be after Turd Eyes delivered his mission statement in the pouring rain to the whole of A Flight. Getting wetter by the minute, it became increasingly difficult to perform his drill commands. Then it started, with no warning. "What the fucking hell did I ever do to deserve such a fucking collection of shit-for-brains no-fucking-hopers as you lot?" I've got just three fucking weeks left to turn a collection of fucking brainless arseholes into the very best airmen ever to leave here. It's not just fucking difficult. It's fucking impossible. But I've done it before and I'll fucking do it again. But be fucking warned. If at the fucking end you're not the very best fucking Flight to parade before the Air Officer Commanding, I'll fucking re-flight all of you so far back, you'll be presenting arms with fucking bows and fucking arrows. And I don't fucking care how fucking long it takes."

Back in the billet and waiting to be marched to the mess for lunch, nobody spoke. But like me, they were shocked and visibly shaken. Up to this time in our training programme, I firmly believed we, collectively, had done our best to please. We had arrived at a place we didn't like in the hands of sadists we didn't like. To do things none of us had ever done before. Heavily punished when things went wrong, disciplined with little or no let up. Day after day, night after night. There were now twenty-eight of us left in A Flight. Alan McBride, who had haggis for brains – possibly the reason his fists did his talking for him. He was a very big, six-foot-plus lad and fearless with it. He'd decided the assault course was, in his broad Gorbals accent, "A piece of piss." It wasn't, and ignoring the advice given by those who knew best, I was told he had fallen and broken his ankle. I was further told he was in hospital and would be until long after our passing-out parade. Once recovered, he was then likely to be transferred to a new squad of recruits, all drilling with bows and arrows, commencing square-bashing all over again. Turd Eyes true to his word. Not so said Bunny to anybody who cared to listen. He'd been told McBride did it purposefully in the hopes he would be invalided out of the RAF. Perhaps someone should have told Bunny that truth cannot lie. That evening, whilst everyone was busy 'bulling' (polishing) their kit, we discussed Turd Eyes' morning outburst. We all agreed after five weeks of blood, sweat and tears, we deserved some encouragement at least. Not the accusations made. The consensus of opinion was that, for the three weeks remaining, we would give Turd Eyes one hundred and ten percent. Nothing he could castigate us for. Just before the pass-out parade. It was a promise I wished I'd never made.

The Lee Enfield 303 rifle and I never became a comfortable couple. The opposite in fact. It was heavy and cumbersome in drill moves. So much so, once too often it nearly slipped from my grasp. The recoil when firing live ammunition left painful bruises on my shoulder and I had an oft-repeated premonition that I would drop the bloody thing in the presence of you-know-who. There were half a dozen who shared my problems. All of us known to Turd Eyes, who was just waiting for one of us to drop his rifle. Whenever he took us for rifle drills, he continually made dire verbal threats as to what would happen to the culprit who did. Every time he did I prayed to God it would not be me. In winter, my exposed extremities quickly became painfully cold.

On this bitterly cold, fateful morning, Turd Eyes decided we would have a full passing-out parade dress rehearsal. It was early winter and heavily frosty. I suffer with poor circulation and by the time we arrived at the present-arms salute drill, my hands were very cold – so cold I almost dropped my rifle, catching it by the barrel just before it hit the deck. There was no noisy clatter. But this was my Achilles heel, I was seconds behind the rest of the squad in completing the drill. I hoped he hadn't seen what had happened, but I knew he had. I looked up and there he was, bearing down on me at one hell of a rate of knots. He stopped just as the slashed peak of his hat caressed the bridge of my nose. By then, I was standing in the present arms position, with the offending rifle held rigidly in front of me. As he started to shout, the first of a shower of spittle was transferred from his mouth onto my chin. Accompanied by the foulest smelling breath, which automatically made me turn my head. "Don't fucking move when I'm addressing you," were his opening remarks. "You fucking did that on fucking purpose, didn't you, you fucking GOON?" I was still standing rigidly to attention, a position from which I only had to bring my rifle butt up hard and fast and he'd be wearing his genitalia as earrings. "Do you know what a fucking GOON is? It's a fucking great big, black, ugly fucking bird that flies backwards across the fucking desert and shits fucking pyramids. You're on a fucking charge first thing in the fucking morning." With that, he dismissed me from the parade, ordered me to hold my rifle above my head and begin doubling around the parade ground. Soon after I started, a thought entered my head. If Bunny Whelan's continual use of profanities exposed his very limited vocabulary, then Turd Eyes was surely qualified to become Chief Executive Officer of the Tourette's Syndrome.

In the morning, I was paraded before the duty officer to answer Hodgson's charges. I was found guilty on all charges Turd Eyes had levelled against me and sentenced to fourteen days cook-house fatigues. Without doubt, he was an out and out bastard. Easy to hate. Impossible to like. His only ambition: every eight weeks to turn untold raw recruits into the very best airmen first class. Bar none. Indifferent to the suffering he caused. His final action was to march them to the station, timed perfectly to arrive just minutes before the train. Exactly what happened to us.

Ever since early breakfast we wondered just what little surprises he was planning. We were soon to find out. We were told that we would be marched to the station. This was not unusual, but we could not understand why we were to be formed up in parade order so bloody early. As no explanation was given we assumed this was to be Turd Eyes' fond farewell. That was until we marched into the railway station. There, in the forecourt, was the biggest heap of A Flight's personal belongings piled high. And, having been marched through the town first, we arrived with just minutes before the train pulled in. We didn't wait for Turd Eyes' dismissal. Every man intent on going home just made a dash for the pile of suitcases. I identified mine quite quickly by its colour, but so many couldn't. How many airmen, frantically searching for their kit, missed the train? I imagine more than a few. Would I be right in thinking Turd Eyes had the last laugh?

ELEVEN

Can you believe she returned letters I produced because the full stops had been typed too heavily? The great difference in our ranks meant there was little I could do, until the last six months of my service. I'll tell you later how it all changed.

Having been accepted to train as a shorthand typist, I was posted to Creden Hill, in Hereford. To my surprise, there was one other male applicant, Tommy Stern by name. He had spent the previous two years as a cub reporter on the *Kentish Mercury*. He loved the job. Delighted he was able to successfully apply for the same course as me. For the same reasons as me. We quickly became the best of mates. Cast adrift in a sea of femininity – a class of WRAFs. Keen to pay homage to our masculine attributes. None were beautiful. Few scarcely attractive. All there to fight for our favours, eight hours a day, the length of the twelve-week course. This was my theory but, in truth, I couldn't have been so badly wrong. And nor could they! In their eyes, Tommy and I were a brace of gays. Or why else would we have successfully applied to join a course universally prepared for women? When the truth became known, hostilities gave way to friendship.

Our time in Creden Hill, Hereford, passed quickly. I found shorthand exceptionally difficult – the typewriter keyboard a visible hardship for would-be left-handed students. You will have gathered that, with this handicap, I just about scraped through the qualification exams. I believe the serious shortage of shorthand typists applying for overseas postings swayed the exam judges' opinion. But here I was, a fully qualified shorthand typist awaiting my posting to Germany. Tommy got the UK posting he asked for, having never wanted to leave England. Consequently it was a short-lived but highly amusing friendship. We enjoyed our time together before the inevitable parting fell due. Not just from Tommy. Also the lovely lassies of Creden Hill.

Now that we were trade-qualified airmen, we were allowed to wear civvies (civilian clothes) on camp when off duty, when and wherever we wished. The same applied to leaving camp during our free time. Twelve weeks of the course under our belts. Accompanied by countless pints of Scrumpy Jack and the few local lassies prepared to befriend lonely airmen, we knew exactly where we were going and where Hereford's 'trendies' hung out. Having been castigated as a brace of gays by the ladies on our course, tonight we were determined to pin our 'randy' flag to the local lassies' masts. We were both hoping this night would be friendly and touchy-feely, before our 23.59 hour curfew brought the curtain down. It wasn't difficult breaking back into camp. And who knew? Should touchy-feely lead to kissy-kissy and exploration of female pastures new, we were ready, willing and able. Two contented airmen, joining the birds in the dawn chorus, singing the praises of the darling ladies of Wales as we wended our weary way home.

We knew from previous visits that far too many Hereford girls kept Creden Hill airmen at arm's length. Why, you may ask. I truly believe they knew the rates of pay for all RAF ranks from top to bottom. From group captain down to leading aircraftmen. They knew that we were bottom of the wealth league. Therefore, our rate of drinking, by necessity, was abnormally slow. They knew our money would expire before the evening did and so stayed politely frigid. Previous visits revealed Welsh girls also crossed the border into Hereford and they weren't shy when it came to sharing the cost of an evening. They were upmost in our thoughts as the bus dropped Tommy and me close to the pub. Our target for tonight? Two lively Welsh lassies, generous with their favours and the odd pint or three. Fingers crossed, eyes roving, money at the ready, we pushed our way to the bar.

We'd hardly crossed the pub threshold and there they were – four lively girls, intent on having a good time. We knew from their accents they were indeed Welsh. I was immediately attracted to Megan as she returned my smile with interest. She was brunette and blessed with a fuller figure – plus an exciting cleavage crying out to be explored and caressed. In no time at all, Tommy and I were in a very close foursome. It was almost as though we had known each other a lifetime. We moved to a vacated table, where legs very soon became intertwined. Along with the cider, the conversation flowed, but sadly, so did the clock. It was a bloody long walk back to Creden Hill and we dare not miss the last bus. They had the same problem in returning to Monmouth. Earlier, Tommy had mentioned how much he missed his mother's Sunday roast lunches and I agreed. I also knew I just had to see Megan again. Soon it became an argument as to whose mum cooked the best Sunday nosh. It was then that the girls had to leave to catch their last bus. We walked them back to the bus depot. I told Megan I hoped to see her again. "Would tomorrow be OK? You can come to lunch. Mum and Dad love to meet my friends." The surprise invitation was graciously accepted, followed by a short, passionate snog. Then they were gone. Leaving two expectant leading aircraftmen praying tomorrow would soon arrive. Happy in the knowledge that, whatever else happened, home-cooked Sunday lunch was an unexpected pleasant surprise assured.

The Sunday-morning bus journey to Monmouth

was agonisingly slow. The conversation was mainly recounting events of the night before. And who would get his end away first. After what seemed like ages, we finally arrived at our destination. There were the girls, sheltering under their umbrellas, looking anxiously as the bus finally came to a halt. It was twelve thirty and time for a pint before lunch. Both Tommy and I were shattered when the girls pointed out we were in Wales and pubs were forbidden to open on Sundays. So it was off to meet Ted and Vera, Megan's mum and dad.

The moment we walked through the door we were instantly made to feel at home. We were given a brace of pints of Ted's renowned home-brewed 'Scrumpy'. Not wishing to offend our host, other than me having a strong desire to bed his daughter, we both did as we were told. Two pints downed in double quick time. To say it was an acquired taste would be an injustice to Ted's brewing prowess. Never before had I tasted the likes of Ted's potent brew. As it caressed my tonsils, my whole body stiffened. Whilst I have neither smelt nor tasted embalming fluid, this, I am sure, was the closest I would ever come to doing so. As for Tommy, had he not been seated, it was odds on he would have fallen over. Ted was delighted with our reaction to his Scrumpy and was pouring two refills. Having done so, he started to sing. All the time we were imbibing, Vera and the girls were busy tasting the new batch of homemade wine, another of Ted's long-practiced brewing achievements. Then it suddenly dawned on me. Whilst I was still just about capable of sensible conversation when asked, Ted told me he had been home-brewing for the best part of twenty-five years. They had found it worked wonders when bottle-feeding Megan and her brother during troublesome nights. Friends and family had encouraged him to experiment with different home-brewed beer, cider and wine. Having done so, they were happy to buy quite large amounts of their particular fancy. Most of which was drunk on Sundays. Purely by chance, Ted had discovered a most enjoyable source of a second income, and an answer well suited to combating Sunday closing. Without doubt, all present on this most enjoyable Sunday, were in various stages of intoxication. Added to which, Ted, being Welsh, like all Welshmen, loved to sing. Singing was also a passion of mine, so I joined him whenever I knew the song he was singing. Everyone was singing except Tommy, who had a voice he didn't deserve. It sounded like Tiny Tim imitating a braying donkey. Whenever he joined in, the rest of us burst into uncontrollable laughter. Suddenly Vera, struggling to get to her feet, loudly exclaimed she was about to wet herself. And what's more, she hadn't made her special gravy for lunch. When asked why was it special, she fled from the room crying, "Wait and see if you can spot what the special ingredient is."

This put me on my guard and I made a mental note to sniff the gravy before introducing it to my Welsh lamb roast. Perhaps introducing unnamed special ingredients to gravy is not unusual in Wales. I daren't ask for fear of upsetting two wonderful hosts and spoiling the best Sunday afternoon I'd had in a very long time. Ted and Vera retired after what had proved to be a most delightful lunch, whatever the magic gravy ingredient was. If the Welsh could make delicious bread out of seaweed, why shouldn't they flavour their gravy in whatever way they chose? With mum and dad no longer present, Megan and I indulged in some serious petting. A most enjoyable ending to one of the strangest weekends ever. Shared with a boozy Welsh family, the likes of which I was sadly never to meet again.

With only days left before I was to sit both shorthand and typing exams, it was doubtful I would do well enough to pass both. I comfortably gained the typing pass rate with flying colours, but not so shorthand, which I could sit again. Or I could remuster as an administrative typist. This I did and was duly posted to Buckeberg, this being the personnel disposal centre for the Second Tactical Air Force, as we were known in Germany. It being Sunday, there was little to do whilst awaiting my final RAF posting in a country whose defeated population despised us being there. So I joined two others, also waiting to be told whereabouts in Germany they were heading. We decided to take a trip into town. And there, whilst window shopping, I very nearly left myself wide open for court martial proceedings being taken against me.

Buckeberg was little more than a large village with a main shopping street. As we slowly started to walk from the top end, I noticed a jewellers on the opposite side of the road. Having decided some time ago to buy a silver-plated cigarette case, I decided to cross over to window shop. I could see my two colleagues not far behind. Being Sunday, the street was practically deserted. The jewellers' window contained virtually everything it should. Everything, that is, except any sign of a cigarette case. I took little notice of the man and his dog sharing the pavement with me. That was until the dog came up to me, wagging his tail furiously.

My love of animals supersedes all else. Stroking this friendly canine, I failed to hear the approach of his master – that is, until he punched me into the gutter. I was shocked more than hurt and couldn't understand a word of what this irate German was screaming at me. The one thing registering in my mind was that we had won the bloody war, not this raving lunatic. By now I was getting to my feet, intent on punching his lights out. If the punch I threw had landed, that's where I would have left him – back in the gutter, where he belonged. But I was stopped in mid-flight and grabbed from behind. I instantly thought he wasn't alone, but accompanied by friends. But I was wrong. It was Ron Warrington-Smith, a fellow leading aircraftman. He marched me away from the fracas that never was, all the time explaining the trouble I would be in for striking a German national, whatever the prevailing circumstances. When we returned to posting HQ, we found we had the same posting. RAF Sylt, one of a group of Frisian Islands on the Danish-German Border. We didn't know it then, but pre-war Sylt was a major holiday resort with nude beaches. A brilliant ideal posting for a red-blooded, horny eighteen year old airman.

I had never met an enigma in my life before. Then along came Ronald Warrington-Smith, aged twenty three. He thought the recruitment authorities had forgotten he existed. So much so he quit working on cruise ships and had, for the past year, worked in area sales management for an international perfume company. Ron still believed someone blew the whistle to the National Service authorities. So here he was. An embittered conscript serving his time. Five years older than me. He was desperate to return to Blighty and the job he loved. Whilst it seemed we had little in common save the RAF uniform we both wore, our growing friendship was there for all to behold. Public-school educated, in his time spent at sea, Ron had visited places I could only dream of. But here I was, sitting next to Ron as our train sped to RAF Sylt. I was to report to Flight Lieutenant Jill Oram, the camp adjutant and my new boss. I was not sure about Ron, who was some sort of flight mechanic. When not working, we spent a great deal of time together.

RAF Sylt was a major base for German flying boats until the war ended. It was then decided it was ideally situated for training novice and newly commissioned RAF fighter pilots in the intricacies of air-to-air combat. Fully operative by the time Ron and I arrived, each month, pilots from other RAF stations in Germany arrived at Sylt. For the next month, they were engaged in a concentrated training programme of air-to-air attack. What they learned in the classroom they were able to practise over the North Sea. Sylt's host pilots would fly over the sea ranges towing drogues (large banners) and the guest pilots would use 60 mm live cannon shells with coloured war heads. They had been taught when to commence their attacks and, critically, to break away at 2,000 yards – the minimal safety distance protecting the Sylt host drogue-towing pilots flying the slower single-seater Tempests. When the attacks ceased, the towing pilots headed for the dropping zone on Sylt and released the drogues. These were collected by ground crew and the number of different coloured hits totalled – each attacking pilot had different coloured cannon ammunition warheads registering hits on the drogues – and the visiting camp with the biggest number of hits on target would win the annual Duncannon Trophy. Winning it was paramount and the competition fierce. Consequently, the young, excited, inexperienced visiting pilots were often high on adrenalin and would forget the attacking break-off safety distance. Finally ending their attacks well short of 2,000 yards. Those guilty got a severe bollocking on landing. Incidentally, something to bear in mind, if there are any readers prepared to take the risk, the ammunition used was 60 mm cannons. If someone was to accurately pin-point the actual North Sea firing ranges, the sea bed would be covered in shell cases of used ammunition. There were literally thousands upon thousands of shell cases ejected during the air-to-air attacks and each cartridge case was copper. A veritable fortune waiting to be harvested. But then again, it may already have been, as it was sixty-seven years ago when I was a towed-target operator.

Ron and I arrived on RAF Sylt along with quite a few of the month's young visiting air-attack pilots. We didn't realise it at the time, but one of the airborne target-towing Tempests was in difficulties. It was low on fuel and could not bring its wheels down to land. Once the gathered pilots realised the problem, they offered helpful remarks such as, "piss in the hydraulics" and "land in the sea and see if she floats." They seemed to think the situation was hilarious. However, they had the decency to applaud when the pilot eventually executed a difficult emergency 'wheels up' landing. After the welcoming excitement, we reported to reception and were allocated our quarters. I was to share a room with two others, both of whom were soon due to return to the UK awaiting demob. Ron's accommodation was similar but on the other side of the parade ground. Home sweet home for the next twenty months!

TWELVE

It was six years since Germany had surrendered and the war in Europe ended. Slowly, Sylt was rebuilding its pre-war reputation as a popular holiday resort for wealthy German families. Plus well-heeled sugar-daddy German businessmen with their young, attractive ladies. During the summer months, large sections of the beach were clearly marked in German, "For Nudists Only", which encouraged visiting pilots, from various other stations to perform low-flying beach antics on their return to base – delighted when their Sylt air-to-air attack training month arrived – much to the chagrin of holidaying Germans. They continuously resented being reminded they hadn't won the war. We did! And when they complained about the continuous aircraft noise, plus the numbers of male airman invading the beaches, it was pointed out that none of us could read or understand German. Should you go to Sylt for your holiday, you will find the beaches littered with large holes. Being North Sea beaches, there is usually a chilling breeze blowing inland. So, the German holiday makers dug quite large, deep holes as protection for their families. And having dug it, they'd place their name in pebbles around it. Woe betides anyone who invades their space!

At the end of the air-to-air attack training, the visiting RAF squadron would return to its German base. Once departed, the new group of trainees would take their place. This was scheduled over the final weekend of the month's training and it usually meant the resident Sylt personnel had the opportunity of spending that weekend on the beach – weather permitting. There were eight of us on this particular weekend, making ourselves comfortable in a large, deep hole vacated by the German family Dongowski. Holiday over, they had since returned home. The summer sun was getting warmer by the hour as we scanned the beach for naked female flesh. Suddenly, Phil 'Woody' Woodman, who happened to be standing, said, with a deep intake of breath, "Fuck me, would you look at that." Seven heads turned as one. Seven pairs of eyes, focused on what he had seen. There, coming straight towards us, was a delightfully lovely young female. Heading straight for our occupied hole. She stopped no more than twenty yards from our sanctuary, topless and wearing the smallest pair of briefs you ever did see. By now, she was fully aware of who we were, turned her back and slowly removed her dazzlingly white briefs before donning even smaller yellow bikini bottoms. She had an absolutely divine bottom. It was then that seven aroused, rampant airmen turned on their fronts in unison, attempting to hide their masculine embarrassment by thrusting each of their excited members in the soft sand. But not Woody. He was transfixed, fully aroused and on his knees. "Christ," he croaked. "She's heading up the beach towards us now." I had never before seen Woody's member, now standing proudly to attention. Nor had anybody else. Prepared and ready for action. It was enormous – like a baby's arm grasping an apple. The looks on the faces of the rest of us ranged from disbelief to envy. Woody was dragged back into our shelter, she was indeed heading straight towards us. I was still in shock, having seen Woody's todger for the very first time. From that day forward he would always be known to me as Happy Harry Hampton.

Those of us who could raise our heads over the edge of our captured hole without embarrassment awaited her arrival. She was still topless but was now wearing the briefest of brief bikini bottoms. In her right hand she held an unlit small cheroot. She had the voice of an angel and a smile to match. She was an absolute stunner. "Hello. I think I've left my lighter back in the hotel. Could I have a light please?" she asked in near-perfect English. In an instant, eight hands, grasping an array of lighters and Swan Vesta matches, were thrust in her direction. At first, conversation was stilted, understandably so as she was topless and very close to bottomless. At this point, we invited her to share a beer and join us in our newly acquired home and out of the chill wind. Remarkably, she did so, despite each one of us being stark-bollock naked. Her name was Eva. She was Polish, twenty-two years old and living in Stuttgart with her 'uncle'. She explained he was a leading German industrialist and chief executive officer of a large manufacturing group of companies. Eva was his favourite niece, who, so she said, he looked after exceedingly well. We wondered exactly what favours she needed to bestow upon her most generous benefactor to satisfy his desires. But not one of us had the balls to ask if our surmisings were correct. It was then Happy Harry Hampton became restless and started to fidget, then bounce. Hoping to hide his embarrassment from Eva, he made a mad dash for the sea, inviting us all to join him. Eva thought this a great idea. Quickly stepping out of her bikini bottoms, she chased Woody to the water's edge. In order to protect our manhood, seven bare, leading aircraftmen, with not a swimming costume between them, followed suit. That was a great mistake, knowing how cold water affects man's best friend. While Eva swam, we splashed about just long enough for her to have seen us. And for Woody to relieve himself. Then, as to a man, seven shrivelled Hampton-owning airmen made a dash for the safety of their captured hole. Having enjoyed her swim, she came to say goodbye. She was meeting her 'uncle' for lunch at the hotel, then they were returning to Stuttgart, leaving eight young men alone with their thoughts. That is, all except Woody. Pleased with his stolen, prized memento of that most unexpected but exceptional day. With a broad grin, he unrolled his towel and produced Eva's yellow bikini bottoms.

THIRTEEN

With one year of my National Service left to serve, I could see no reason why Sylt wouldn't remain my home from home. I was happy with my lot, all bar one. From our very first meeting in flying wing HQ, I was on edge. My boss was a female flight lieutenant – who wore her delusions of grandeur on her sleeve for all to see. Why? Probably because she was the PA to Wing Commander Clementi, the station commandant and most important officer on camp. My boss was a 'plain Jane', with thin lips and a prominent hook-nose. She was decidedly overweight and chunky with it. I immediately thought her only chance of being bedded was as a raffle prize. Her name was Jill Oram, but she insisted I addressed her by her rank.

She regularly pointed out she had specifically asked UK postings to send her a female shorthand typist and how disappointed she had been when she got me. Whilst I will be the first to admit my shorthand was rubbish, I believed practice could have made it better. But it was never forthcoming. She employed me as a copy typist. No more, no less. When I asked why, she practically accused me of insubordination for questioning her decision. Flight Lieutenant Jill Oram and I had long since realised we shared a mutual dislike of each other. Especially when she started to return my typing, claiming my punctuation, especially full stops, were being typed too heavily. That for me was the final straw. If and when a more suitable opportunity arose, I would apply for it. If successful, I would happily take leave of the only permanent pain in the arse causing me grief.

Once you had accepted Sylt was not typical of the rest of Germany, you could sit back and appreciate the good things on offer. As I have already said, once the holiday season had passed, the locals quickly realised RAF Sylt was here to stay. So they decided to befriend us once winter arrived. On camp, our social centre was a well-appointed NAAFI. It provided an answer to most of our needs and the prices were sympathetic to the limited weekly incomes of almost all of us. It was used nightly by both airmen and WRAFs alike. Whatever your social interests, most would be shared by others. As an example, Woody and I shared a love of jazz. He returned from his first UK leave with a portable record player and a varied jazz record collection. I did the same with my jazz collection. For a couple of evenings a week, we would hold NAAFI jazz requests.

It didn't take long before we had quite a few regular followers. During an evening in Sylt, Woody discovered the wonderful American Stan Kenton's big band was playing the Ernst Merk Halle in Hamburg. It was their first ever European tour and probably the only opportunity we would get of seeing the great man and his world number-one premier big jazz band. When we told our jazz night followers the news, eight, including two girls, decided they would love to see them too. They left Woody and me to make all the arrangements, including overnight arrangements and tickets. I asked Gunter Shultz, my office companion, if he could help, as my ability to speak German was pathetic. He took over and the weekend was superb.

As I have said, there were other groups of varied interests. All of which used the NAAFI for meetings, which gave me the idea of a Sylt newsletter. It would be published quarterly and contain news from the different camp interest groups that met regularly. Plus, news of town events, the Duncannon Trophy league, news from home, updates on UK football teams/leagues and sport in general, poems, stories and articles from camp personnel. Rather than discuss with Jill Oram, I went straight to Wing Commander Clementi. He was not too sure at first, but warmed to the idea when shown the letter and article I had received from the manager of Newcastle United Football Club regarding the Argentinian brothers Robledo, both of whom now played for his club. The station commander said I could use the small office located in the building housing the station heating system. It was small but fit for purpose. Especially as it was the middle of winter and it was both quiet and beautifully warm. Whilst I was speaking with him, he brought up the worsening situation between Jill Oran and me. I told him the truth, explaining my situation and that it was, in my honest opinion, unresolvable. And that she would not be happy until she had an aircraftwoman in my place. I went on to ask him if it were true that we were soon to replace our squadron of battered old Tempests with modern Meteor 8 aircraft. If so, could I be considered for one of the towed-target operators to work alongside the Meteor pilots. As I left his office, he promised to consider my request.

FOURTEEN

On this particular evening, Woody's NAAFI Jazz Club had gathered a dozen or so followers, amongst whom was Aircraftwoman Pearl Morgan. She showed great interest as I explained the camp newsletter and how I envisaged its quarterly content. I knew little of her, only that she was a petite Yorkshire lass and quite pleasing on the eye. Normally, when she came to the NAAFI, she was accompanied by the same bloke, who I took to be her boyfriend. But not so on this occasion. She was a long-term senior aircraftwoman now in her third year and had been serving on Sylt for twenty months. She knew the island well and would be a good correspondent for the newsletter, covering all things WRAF. She instantly agreed when I posed the question. So, there and then, I asked if she would like to see where all things newsletter happened. She said she would love to.

It was bitterly cold as we left Woody and his jazz devotees in the NAAFI. As we crossed the frozen parade ground, Pearl commented on how very cold it was. We unlocked my small newsletter office door and were enveloped by a cloud of comforting warmth. Almost immediately, Pearl took off her top coat as I turned to close the door.

"Can you come here any time you like?" she asked.

"Indeed I can and do," I replied. "Probably because not many people on camp know of its existence."

"You lucky bugger," she retorted. "It's the warmest I've been this winter." She then asked me when the first newsletter would be finished and ready for circulation. I told her it should be ready in six weeks and asked if she would like to see the dummy layout. I passed it to her and turned my attention to the article I had received that weekend from the manager of Newcastle United Football Club. They had recently signed the Robledo brothers from Argentina and I wanted to know why, and if they were happy playing football in England. Pearl had remained quiet so far so I turned to ask her if there was anything she wanted. Her answer was: "Yes. You."

As she started to remove her sweater, she said, "It's so lovely and warm. Why don't you join me?" I needed no second asking as her sweater came off, exposing young tip-tilted breasts waiting to be admired and caressed. It then dawned on me. All the time she expressed interest in my newsletter, it was a ploy to add me to an ever-growing list of conquests. She was a good friend of Woody's, who had told her of my idea to produce a camp newsletter, and the facilities provided. Also that he believed I was a virgin. Why, I don't know and I was angry. But as soon as I cupped both delightful breasts in my hands, he was forgiven. As she removed my baggy RAF pants, she took full control of our love-making. We made love twice and I felt I had acquitted myself well. It was as we dressed that she told me she had applied for and been granted a new Far East posting. She had four weeks UK leave and then it was goodbye to Sylt for good. Having stolen my virginity, she left, taking it with her. I had just two regrets: she would not be around to report on WRAF activities for the newsletter and I thought I had found a willing partner to share my sexual desires until I left Sylt. I was unhappy about both, until the very next day, when my TTO appointment was confirmed.

I had never felt so cold as I did in Sylt in mid-winter. Then, that is not surprising, as the sea in Amrum bay, where our air/sea rescue launch was kept, would freeze. It happened every year and was replaced by a helicopter and crew. The incumbent RAF squadron's four-week air-combat training over, they were pulling out that weekend. At the same time, we awaited the helicopter pilot and ground crew's arrival from the UK. The RAF Celle air-attack squadron having departed, flying was stood down. It so happened Sunday was Flight Lieutenant Ian Cooper, the helicopter pilot's, birthday. Our native pilot attack instructors decided he was worthy of a birthday party in the officers' mess. He was flattered and considered it an honour. With strong German lager at just sixpence a pint, the pints kept coming and Ian kept sinking them. When the party ended, he was well and truly blathered. He thanked his hosts, said goodbye and returned to his quarters. Or so thought the Sylt home crew. Drunk or sober, not one of them could have known what was to follow later that afternoon. Nobody could. And, as I wasn't there, I can only relate what happened as it was told to me.

Soon after arriving on Sylt, complete with helicopter, Ian was delighted to see Sally Yeomen, a senior aircraftwoman he had known from a previous UK posting. In the short space of time they had known each other, they had become good friends. Once she knew Ian was a helicopter pilot, she made him promise to give her a flight if ever the opportunity arose. It never did before Sylt. Sally was unexpectedly posted away and Ian lost touch. He was delighted when he discovered Sally had in fact been transferred to Sylt from the UK. At that time, Ian was supporting the RAF Regiment manoeuvres in Ireland. On his return, three months later, Sally was gone. Much to Ian's disappointment. Now, their friendship reinstated, Sally reminded Ian of his promise to take her for a trip in his helicopter. As practice air-combat flying was stood down, he told her he would do so that weekend. And to bring a couple of friends with her.

He knew he wasn't totally sober when he left to meet

Sally. It was cold, raining and heavily overcast. This was reason enough to cancel the flight. But when he saw Sally and her three friends huddled under umbrellas, he felt he could not let her down again. So he would make it a short trip around the island. He quickly ushered the girls on board, did the necessary instrument checks and was soon airborne. This, I understood, would be normal procedure every time he flew. He then circumnavigated Sylt at low height. Because of lousy weather, they had poor visibility. They had been airborne about twelve minutes when Ian told the girls he was heading back to the landing pad. What happened next was a disaster. According to the girls, he hovered close to HQ's clock tower, threatening to alter the hands of the big clock. They thought he was joking, but apparently he was not. That's when he lost control and the helicopter suddenly reared upright and slammed into the HQ building. Still drunk, he managed to open the door before he cut the controls.

The helicopter came to rest standing upright on its tail, leaning against the clock tower. The girls started to scream, struggling to get to the door, whilst a shocked Ian just sat at the controls. He repeated over and over again: "I'm sorry, I'm sorry." In no time at all, camp personnel gathered, wondering what the hell was going on. Someone had the foresight to raise the alarm and the station fire tender was quickly on site. The fire crew swiftly had the extendable ladder in place and Sally and friends vacated the chopper with all speed and were soon back on terra firma.

Not so Ian. Whilst Sally swore never to board a helicopter again, he steadfastly refused to leave his stricken vessel. When he finally did, they needed to send to the mainland for a mobile crane. It was needed to lift the chopper off the building and lower it to the ground. Within forty-eight hours, Ian was arrested and returned to the UK. There, he had the book thrown at him. He was eventually court martialled and dismissed from the service. Much to the remorse of the Sylt pilots, who admitted getting him legless on his birthday. The new helicopter and pilot replacement were very quickly residing on the vacant helipad, as there could be no air-to-air target flying whilst the air/sea rescue launch remained frozen solid in Amrum bay harbour.

FIFTEEN

Just before I left the island for Christmas leave, news I had been waiting to hear was telegraphed to Flying Wing HQ. It had been rumoured that we were to exchange the squadron of single-seat Tempest aircraft for two-seater Meteor 8s. It gave delivery dates in February and I was thrilled. No doubt Flight Lieutenant Oram was too. I was called into Wing Commander Clementi's office and told I would be one of six volunteers who would re-muster to towed-target operators in January – date to be advised. I was overjoyed. Slightly apprehensive too, knowing once my training was complete, my new duties would mean I would be airborne practically every day. But saying goodbye to Lady Oram, plus extra flying money still to be advised, was reward enough. They were the real bonus. It felt like all my Christmases had come at once, but for one thing. Whilst Christmas at home was every serviceman's dream, it meant boarding the troopship *Wansbeck* twice. There and back. Having already sailed from Holland to England once, I knew what to expect.

The journey home began with a train to Hamburg from Sylt. Being an island, you had to be aware that the causeway rail track was prone to flooding, rather like Mersea in Essex, which is also affected by tides. Once on the Hamburg train, you settled down for a lengthy, boring journey to the Hook of Holland. There you embarked upon an ancient vessel built when comfort was not a prerequisite. Either that or someone forgot to fit stabilisers, or perhaps they were still on the drawing board. Whatever the reason, the *Wansbeck* was a flat-bottomed tub, lovingly re-christened HMS Vomit. Just the slightest swell and the rolling would begin. Now imagine, as she ploughed through the night, that slight swell developing into a force six gale, which it now and again did, especially in winter. Often long before HMS Vomit docked at Harwich. The result, on ordinary service personnel trying to sleep below decks, was horrendous. The sleeping arrangements on the bottom deck comprised bunks, ensuring the maximum use of space available. The first time on board, I couldn't fathom why service personnel began gathering at the top of the steps quite some time before we were due to set sail.

I waited for the curfew to sound before I descended the steep iron stairs. Having investigated the sleeping arrangements earlier, I decided on a top bunk berth. I searched the whole deck but there wasn't one to be found. In the end, I managed to find a middle bunk. Unhappily, it was alongside the engine room which I knew would be very noisy. As indeed it was. But it failed to cushion the noise of those amongst us who were poor sailors. There was only a slight swell throughout the night, but within an hour of sailing, I estimated half the compliment of my soldier and airmen colleagues were unwillingly parting with food they had enjoyed in the past twelve hours. Down every aisle there were countless spirals of technicolour yawns plunging onto the steel clad decks, interspersed by groans and moans from those who cried out – praying death would quickly put an end to their misery. Now you could see why the top bunks were at a premium. They were a much sought after vomit-free guarantee for those in the know.

Whether you were a seasoned sailor or not, there was absolutely no way you would choose to sleep on the bottom of three bunks. Why? In even the slightest of sea swells, you were continually splattered by the vomit of those lying above you. And by the morning, every one of the aisles of three-tiered bunks was running freely with evil-smelling sick. And the bottom bunks were only some eighteen inches from the deck. There was simply no escaping the foul mini tsunamis of overpowering free flowing puke, running back and forth with every roll of the ship. Now, start to imagine what would happen if you encountered a force-six storm. That alone could cause you to throw up. Fortunately, and thanks to my love of sea fishing, I never did. Climbing onto my middle bunk, I prayed to my God in heaven I never would. But there was one advantage. Because the stench stayed with you, customs officers stayed well clear. Knowing that, reasonable smuggling wasn't difficult. I carried the maximum amount of contraband I could, hidden on my person. In four trips to the UK, I was never once searched when we landed. A nice little earner.

The training for my new job of towed-target operator took less than a week. I then had two trips, sitting alongside the pilot, enabling him to assess that I was singularly able to perform my new duties with minimal discomfort. He also threw the Meteor 8 about to test that there were no visible signs of air sickness. I passed both with flying colours. One of the pilots I flew with most of the time was Flight Lieutenant Jones. An excellent pilot attack instructor in whom I had absolute confidence. He was eventually posted back to England, where I was told he was assigned to the Red Arrows, eventually becoming leader of this worldwide-acclaimed aerobatic team. A promotion well deserved, honouring his flying prowess.

I keenly enjoyed performing my new responsibilities well away from the constant nagging of Flight Lieutenant Oram. Admittedly, working days were longer, as we used every last daylight hour for air-attack sorties, but being airborne gave me a new-found sense of freedom. Demob came ever closer, I could practically taste it. But then again, there were times when partnering Jonsey, I considered signing on for a further tour of duty. I would have done so, believing my job as a trainee sports journalist with the *Sunday Pictorial* was guaranteed. Most likely I would have signed on for a further two years, had I known what awaited me just around the corner. Nor would I have written to my mother telling her I would be home for good in three months' time. If I did but know it, I was tempting fate.

No matter which of the three services you were in, ordinary lower-rank personnel have a universal dislike of any type of military police. The reason might well be that, once their training ends, they inherit the rank of corporal. Then, and almost without exception, they abuse the power of their rank, believing they are untouchable. It's an attitude they all wear like a campaign medal. If you're wise, show respect. If sensible, leave well alone. I rigidly followed my own advice. Except this once. They say there is an exception to every rule. On RAF Sylt, his name was Corporal Alan Broadhead. A Lancastrian, cast in a completely different mould. Or so I thought.

SIXTEEN

I should not have let my guard drop.

As flying wing HQ and the military police offices were adjacently positioned, our paths crossed almost daily. From the very beginning, we exchanged polite pleasantries and over time they grew into conversation. I learned a great deal about Alan. His likes and dislikes, family background, why he joined the RAF police. I decided he was too nice a bloke to be a copper and I thought I was a pretty shrewd judge of character. So what the hell was I doing here? Lying in a sea of mud in Colchester military prison, surrounded by lots of bits of Bren gun, having no idea which bits went where. Staring at a sergeant prison 'screw', bearing down on me at a fast rate of knots. I muttered angrily, "Once I'm out of this Colchester shit hole, Broadhead, if our paths ever cross again, you're a dead man."

It was a lovely early September evening and when I saw Alan that morning, he suggested we go for a drink in town. I mentioned it to Ron, but he was on late call servicing one of the drogue-towing Meteor 8s required for the morning's air-attack programme. If he finished on time he said he would join us later. Following dinner, I joined Alan at the main gate and we set off for the RAF club on the outskirts of town, used by both commissioned and non-commissioned officers. They had separate bars of course, but the prices in each were subsidised. Alan explained the draft lager was just sixpence a pint. He told me to fill my boots as it was his treat, explaining I wouldn't be served as I was not a club member.

As the evening drew on, the club gradually filled. I thought I was getting some strange looks from Alan's police colleagues, but thought it was because I was a non-member. Normally when I drank in the camp NAAFI, I stopped at three pints – pint four was the one that did the damage. Tonight, Alan was the perfect host. To this day, I'm still not certain how many pints over my normal limit I had. Nor did I notice he had slowed his consumption down. I was enjoying the evening – he was buying, I was drinking. I'd had more than enough as the curfew hour approached. It was unlikely Ron would join us now. If he had, the evening would have ended so completely differently.

I remember little of the walk back over the airfield. I walked slowly and found it difficult to do so in a straight line. Alan kept close to me, offering help. As he put his arm round me I tripped and fell. I lay there, making no attempt to get to my feet. I drunkenly told him this was to be my bed for the night, turned on my side and closed my eyes. I think he tried to kiss me and at the same time force his hand inside my trousers. It was then I realised he was unbuttoning my trousers. Sitting up, my knee was level with his nose and with all the power I could muster I drove it as hard as I could into his face. Not waiting to see the damage I had done, I scrambled to my feet and fled. I should not have gone straight to my billet, but to the police office and reported what had happened. That I didn't, cost me dearly.

I quickly undressed and got into bed. I lay there in the dark wondering what I should do next. My first thought was to report it to the warrant officer, Alan's police boss. Or even Wing Commander Clementi. But then I was due to be repatriated to the UK in less than five weeks. Then my two-year National Service would be over. Prior to changing my duties to TTO, I'd been an administrative typist for sixteen months – long enough to know just how slowly it would take for my report to be acted upon. It would certainly delay my return to England and Civvy Street. Before I finally closed my eyes I decided to do nothing. That was a mistake. A very foolish mistake. The outcome of which I should have foreseen.

All of Broadhead's police colleagues knew he was gay. Hence the reason I was getting those quizzical looks in the club. Seemingly, he had been warned not to take any of his homosexual conquests to their club. Apparently, when he reported for duty the next morning, his right eye was black and closed; the right side of his face swollen. When questioned, he totally reversed what had happened. He said we were both drunk and it was I that had come onto him. He had refused my advances, whereupon I punched and kicked him. The only truth in the whole of his report was that we were both drunk. Or at least I was – very. I was immediately arrested and confined to a cell. Just before lunch I was questioned by the police warrant officer. He conveniently forgot to tell me there should have been an officer present. The statement I made then was very different to the evidence given later in my court martial.

I was under house arrest and forbidden to leave the camp. I was ordered to report to the guardroom before breakfast, lunch and dinner. But, thanks to Flight Lieutenant Jones I was allowed to continue my duties as a TTO. I still believed Broadhead would tell the truth concerning the events of that fateful evening, the threatening court martial would be dropped and I would be returned and demobbed in the UK. My heart sank when I was re-arrested and detained in the guardroom until the court martial was convened. Flight Lieutenant Tetroe was appointed as my defending officer. He was Canadian and one of the pilot attack officers. If I wasn't flying with Jonesy then my choice would have been Jack Tetroe. We liked each other and I told him all that I could remember, after leaving the club with Broadhead. When finished, he put his arm around my shoulders and said just two words: 'NOT GUILTY.'

That he believed me encouraged me no end. He further pointed out that because of the seriousness of the charges against me, a civilian solicitor had been appointed to defend me. His name was William Hemming. He was an ex-detective sergeant who had studied law whilst a policeman and qualified once he left the force. When we met he immediately put me at my ease. He listened carefully whilst I recounted everything I could remember had happened. Not just during that evening, but from the first moment our paths had crossed. He asked lots of questions and took copious notes. Stared intently at me as he asked me the direct questions, "Are you homosexual?" and "When socialising, do you prefer the company of men rather than women?" He laughed when I explained that Pearl had stolen my virginity a few months earlier. But we would have to search the whole of Yorkshire if we wanted her as a witness. I liked this man a lot. With him and Jack Tetroe defending me, I was sure the truth would out and I would be home for Christmas.

Please understand, all of this happened over sixty-five years ago. I tried desperately hard to leave what happened back in Germany, not wanting the events of that evening to be my constant companion in later life. It was a gross miscarriage of justice, which was later successfully appealed by my civilian lawyer once I had left the Royal Air Force. Consequently, it is truly a thing of the past, memories of which today are no longer easy to recall. The actual court martial lasted two days. As well as Sylt personnel, there were also officers from elsewhere brought into the court to try me. The prosecuting officer was an out and out bastard. The moment my escort and I were marched into court, even before the charges were read out, he decided I was guilty. I was very nervous, standing stiffly to attention behind a chair, utilised as a makeshift dock, whilst he was as regimental as a button stick. From whence he came I know not. Within the first hour of being interrogated, telling the court what, in my drunken state, I remembered of that evening, I knew he was determined to nail me on the charges I faced. Hell bent on proving the RAF police, and indeed the Royal Air Force itself, were whiter than white, could do no wrong. And there was no place in its ranks for vicious homosexuals like me.

He tore me and my statement to shreds. But not the parts which I swore on oath I was seeing and hearing for the first time. He turned virtually everything I said in to mitigation against me. And it was he who informed me that, during my sustained attack on Broadhurst, I had broken his nose. I had lost my temper by this time. Wishing by now and almost shouting that it should have been his bloody neck. I also asked the question, "How do you mount a vicious, sustained attack from a sitting position?" which he totally ignored. But in spite of the valiant defence put forward by my defence lawyer, William Hemming – plus the glowing character references, gathered and put forward by defending officer Jack Tetroe – I left the court with a sinking feeling in the pit of my stomach. I knew it wasn't going well. Far from it.

The only person I hated as much as Broadhead was the prosecuting officer. From the beginning he set out to make sure I lost my temper, which I did on three occasions. Whilst out of court and awaiting the verdict, I remonstrated with myself for being so damn stupid. Both Hemming and Tetroe had strongly warned me of the serious consequences of doing so, especially as this was a military and not a civilian court. But knowing what had really happened, which was not the version of events the court was being asked to accept, nor the character assassination of a vicious, practising, homosexual they did their level best to prove. Unbelievably, they did so on both counts. The next day, the court sentenced me to nine months in Colchester military prison. Also, I was to be discharged with ignominy from the Royal Air Force when I finished my sentence.

I was truly shattered. Dumbfounded. Whatever Tetroe and Hemming said I heard little of. All I heard was a voice sentencing me to a further nine months in uniform, in a place far worse than where it all began, RAF Wilmslow. Before Hemming returned to the UK, he visited me in the guardroom, where I was to be held until escorted to Colchester, which was forty-eight hours later. He said he was shocked with the verdict, calling it a grave miscarriage of justice, and that he intended to appeal the verdicts as soon as he was back in England. God bless him, he was as good as his word.

I was in the fourth week of my sentence and it was absolutely brutal. Soul-destroying. Every screw was hell-bent on making life as difficult and miserable as humanely possible. Army, Navy or Royal Air Force, there was no differentiation between the service you were in, in their eyes you were a guilty, sub-human prisoner, desperately in need of disciplining. From the moment you stepped through Colchester's prison gate, your new life began. Whatever you were found guilty of, they chose the punishment to fit the crime. I kept myself very much to myself. I don't think any one of my fellow prisoners knew of the charges against me. Whenever asked, I told them I was sentenced to nine months for occasioning actual bodily harm on a bully of an RAF copper. This made me some kind of a good bloke, but I knew full well it would not take long for my newly found friends to discover the charges levelled against me. I would then have to watch my back. Every second of every hour I was imprisoned, if not, I was convinced I would be badly hurt. It quite often happened to gay men in those days. The food was barely edible and the portions minuscule. You were deliberately kept hungry. But as unappetising and boringly repetitive as the food was, you were always left wanting more. Once inside Colchester, wherever you went, you did so at the double, often in full kit or holding an Enfield rifle over your head.

Tall or skinny; fat or obese; sick or unwell, it mattered not. You ran until ordered to stop. Only when fit to drop. Shit or shine, you spent many hours on the parade ground, being hard-drilled by unsympathetic prison guards. Wilmslow's drill instructors were pussycats by comparison. The other unbelievable hardship was the assault courses of varying degrees of difficulty. They accounted for many of the injuries, which occurred to prisoners, especially the fat and obese. I hadn't been in Colchester long before I was told what the initial letters of MPSC, the flashes on the shoulders of all military guard uniforms, stood for: Murderers of Poor Sammy Clayton. Some years previously, Colchester had a prisoner by name of Samuel Clayton. Apparently, being fat and way overweight, he should never have been conscripted, but he was. Then, prior to orders for his release from the army finally being given, he was sent to Colchester. There, because of the treatment he received, he died. So the initials MPSC became Murderers of Poor Sammy Clayton. In the little time I had so far spent in Colchester, I found it a plausible story. A fitting explanation describing the daily practice of those currently responsible for running Colchester military prison. As a story it was probably untrue, but, being on the receiving end, it needed little imagination for it to become believable.

Momentarily, looking away from the multitude of Bren gun parts spread over a large area and with no idea how it all fitted back together, I wondered why the police sergeant was deep in conversation with our group instructor. My heart sank as they both started off in my direction and stopped when they reached me. I had no idea what was coming next. The instructor spoke first, "Leading Aircraftman Payne, thirty minutes ago, headquarters received information concerning you. You are to accompany Sergeant Grosvenor back to HQ immediately." I was called to attention and marched, at the double, the 400 yards back to the HQ building. All the way back, I tried to figure out what I had done, but on arrival I still had no idea why I was being ordered to report to the admin block. I had asked Sergeant Grosvenor what it was I had done, but I think, somewhere in his dim, dark past, he had decided never to talk to prisoners and he had no intention of telling me. Waiting in the outer office, my mind in a turmoil, I was close to wishing I had worn a second pair of Y-fronts.

After what seemed an eternity, I was called into the inner office. I believed the seated officer to be a captain, but, having never been good with army ranks, I couldn't be sure. He studied me at length before speaking, then came straight out with it. "We owe you an apology, Payne. What I am about to tell you was received late on Friday. But it was misfiled as 'pending' and not 'urgent' as it should have been." He hesitated, then continued, "the appeal lodged on your behalf by your lawyer, Mr Hemming, was successful on all counts. This means you should have been told forty-eight hours ago. I'm sorry you weren't. Please get all your belongings together and report back here. You'll be given all necessary paperwork, train warrant and money. You are now a free man."

I could not believe what I was hearing. If I had not been sitting down, I think I would have fallen down. As I walked slowly back to my billet, my legs were like jelly, but it was nice and I hardly noticed that no one screamed at me to double. As I gathered all of my belongings together, it dawned on me I would be home for Christmas. And every future Christmas. That made me feel a great deal better. I could not thank Hemming enough. He was indeed true to his word. Together, we had taken on Her Majesty's Armed Forces. And won! There was a car waiting for me when I returned to HQ and in no time at all I was at Colchester station. Once on the train bound for London, I locked myself in the toilet. Why? As one wrongly accused and punished for things abhorrent to me, far too many mistakes had been allowed to happen. Could this be another? If it was and they came to take me back, they would need to search every "thunderbox" on the train first.

SEVENTEEN

My ideal job kicked into touch.

I finally believed I was a free man when I stood staring at the front door of my parents' house in Kidbrooke, south east London. Having written and told my mother I was thinking of signing on for one more year in the RAF, she was delighted when I walked through the front door. I thought it best to explain that I was so happy with my new TTO job, plus I loved flying every day, however, I was told that three years was the minimum I could sign for once my National Service was over. I wasn't happy lying to her, but if I told her the truth, she would have been most upset. As for my step-father, he hardly looked up from the football coupon system he was developing, convinced it was only a matter of time before he won the £75,000 – Littlewoods Pools' first dividend. He told anyone who cared to listen that his name was already on the winning cheque. I told him it was more likely to appear on his gravestone first. As Christmas came and went, I waited to travel to Geraldine House and the *Sunday Pictorial*. Being a national serviceman, they were obliged to offer me a job. My two years obligatory service in the RAF now completed. And I had the papers to prove it.

When I was growing up, I was once told, by someone far wiser than me, the world never stops turning. How true I thought this to be as I entered Geraldine House. The changes began there – the people manning the reception desk were different. Nick Carter, my ex-boss had died unexpectedly, Harold Barker, the managing editor had retired and Hugh Cudlipp appointed in his place. On the picture desk, photographer Bill Turner had retired and Ben Jones was now the art editor of sister paper the *Daily Mirror*. But for me, the news that Peter Thompson, chief soccer reporter, had moved on set alarm bells ringing. Rightly so, as I was convinced, he would have been my champion when meeting with the group human resources manager. She listened while I told her of what had happened prior to my National Service call-up, believing the job of junior sports journalist awaited my return.

She sat and sympathetically listened before explaining there must have been a misunderstanding on my part. In the history of the *Sunday Pictorial*, there had never been junior reporter vacancy, in sport or otherwise. If, during the past two years, I had worked as a local press cub reporter instead of being in the

RAF, it might well have been different. Having gained the necessary experience, I could have applied for a journalistic position had one been available. She went on to say I was probably now too old and inexperienced to be accepted as a cub reporter on most local rags.

She finished the interview by offering me a position in circulation, helping boost sales of the *Pictorial*, soon to be renamed the *Sunday Mirror*. She could see I was bitterly disappointed, and suggested I call her by the end of the week with my decision. As I left her office, I already knew the answer and so did she. Deciding to say farewell to those remaining who I knew, I made my way up to the second floor. I'm so glad I did. By the time I'd said hello and goodbye to one and all, I was ready to leave. I'd spoken to the whole bunch and felt tons better. Especially when Paul Boyle took me to one side. Having got through the greetings bit, he said to me, "If you're still keen on football and not rushing off home, I'd like you to see a good friend. I'll call him now and if he's free he'll see you." He was, and, having thanked Paul profusely, I was on my way. Les Perrin, whose office was just off Charing Cross Road, was the man I was to see. It was not far away, so I decided to walk. In the time it took, I was unable to fathom who Les Perrin was, nor the football problem for whom he needed someone he could trust to help solve it. That's all Paul would say. But no sooner was I on my way, than Paul rang him again and gave him a glowing character reference on my behalf.

EIGHTEEN

I was none too impressed with the office I eventually found. It was so small, I believed Les Perrin to be a sufferer of dwarfism. You climbed two flights of dimly lit stairs, arriving at a closed door which bore the following handwritten note, "Perrins' Penthouse. If you've brought a bottle, enter. If not, don't." I did, without a bottle. My mind now very much at ease, I immediately thanked him for seeing me at such short notice. The small office was sparsely furnished: just one ancient, battered desk and two equally decrepit chairs. He introduced himself, asking me to call him Les. Thanks to Paul Boyle he knew quite a lot about me, particularly about my time with the *Sunday Pictorial* prior to my RAF call-up. He closely questioned me about my football knowledge. It was about now that I began to understand the answers he gave to the questions I asked. My confidence was growing.

Answering the next question from Les led me to believe this was a job I wanted. He said he had a problem, but not enough time to solve it. He asked if I knew anything about the Kirchin Big Band. I answered no, but what was their interest in football? It appears Basil Kirchin's son Ivor had left his father's band to start his own. Now complete, their first engagement was in Nottingham in three weeks' time. Les had only recently set up his promotions company and was totally immersed in launching Ivor Kirchin's Big Band's first gig at the Nottingham town hall. As a new publicity and PR company with the usual set up costs, he was actively seeking new accounts. He was beginning to get good launch press coverage in the music, entertainment, family and local press for the new band's Nottingham launch. With a long-term contract in the offing, you can understand why Les was giving it his full attention. And that's where I came in.

A good friend of his with strong sporting contacts in the Russian Embassy was asked to recommend a reliable UK publicist, who would be needed to work with a Russian football team who would be touring the UK in six weeks. Being a good friend, he knew Les was actively seeking new accounts, so he asked the question: was he interested? His answer: indeed, he was. That agreed, he was called to the embassy, where he made a successful pitch and came away with the business. While all this was going on, he knew nothing of Ivor Kirchin's new band – it came out of the blue without warning. Being on his own and having to travel the country with the Moscow Dynamos, he knew he was facing an impossible situation. That was unless he found reliable help. He discussed his problem over an evening drink with Paul Boyle and two days later I saw Paul when visiting the *Sunday Pic*. The rest, you know.

The Moscow Dynamos and me. Unbelievable. Unthinkable. I wanted to tell everybody sitting in the carriage on my train journey home. Before I left Les, he handed me all the details of their four-game UK tour which was just weeks away. Their first game was against Wolverhampton Wanderers; Liverpool just one week later. Les said he would open an upfront expense account to cover hotel, living and other incidental expenses whilst I was away from home. He was writing to his contact in the Russian Embassy, introducing me in my tour-troubleshooting role. We were to meet when the team arrived in England, but in the meantime I was to contact each of the hotels booked, making sure they understood what was required of them and confirming every detail requested by the Russian Embassy was understood and would be made available to the Russians on their arrival. My responsibilities during the tour were many, but from the start I loved the opportunity Les had given me, vowing I would carry them out to the last detail. The final game was to be played at Wembley, then the Moscow Dynamos team and entourage would up-sticks and return to Russia, via the Russian Embassy. Les hoped they would prepare a report on how well I'd acted in ensuring everything went smoothly and how well or otherwise I handled problems, which were bound to occur. I sensed this would influence my future working alongside him.

There was an awful lot of responsibility resting on my young shoulders. I wasted no time in calling all of the hotels, together with the other teams the Russians would be playing. I was to join them at their hotel and accompany them to each match. I would no doubt meet Billy Wright, the Wolves and England captain, and his wife, then one of the world-renowned three singing sister group, the Beverley Sisters. I imagined I would enjoy the same or similar treatment with the three other opposing top soccer teams. I was ecstatic. All this and I was still just twenty-one years old. I owed it all to Paul Boyle. But neither he nor I foresaw what was soon to happen next.

I made regular reports on my daily activities, which I hoped were impressing Les. I also rang him, usually from the hotels I had so far visited, and especially those who gave cause for concern regarding issues raised by the Russians. I occasionally asked how the promotion for the Kirchin Big Band launch was progressing. Though I did not know it at the time, I was later told Les was renowned for playing his cards close to his chest. In very few words, he told me all was looking good, especially what he had organised one week ahead of the band's appearance. When I asked, he gave a one-word answer, "STUNNING!" Perhaps I should have questioned him more closely. Particularly as I had been told by those who knew him well, he was not afraid of 'sailing close to the wind'. What happened next, nobody, especially Paul and myself, could have foretold in a million years. Sadly, for me, the result was disastrous.

Eventually, Paul gave me the full story. Without telling a soul, Les had arranged a low-flying air drop over the ever-busy shopping centre in Nottingham, just one week before the Kirchin band played a single note. The only other person who knew was a close friend who happened to be a pilot and he would book and fly the two-seater aircraft. The ETA over the drop-zone was 12.30p.m. on the prior Saturday. Basil told his friend they would need to break low-flying regulations, while they flew, emptying the six large sacks of coloured Kirchin leaflets. Mission accomplished, Les calculated, if lucky, they would be there and gone before anybody realised they were flying illegally – directly below established commercial aircraft flight paths.

Those magnificent men in their flying machine would use a two-seater aircraft – one with a floor-level loading bay. On each of their six low-flying runs over the centre of Nottingham, they would empty one of the bags of one thousand leaflets. Once finished, they would climb to the right height and fly with all speed back to the home airfield. Then into their car and beat a swift retreat down the M1 to the relative safety of London. They knew the risk they were taking, but if everything went to plan they believed the Kirchin band launch would be a blast and well worth it. They were right about the launch. It was a sell-out. The new Kirchin Big Band was on its way, but so were the intrepid twosome. To jail. Accused of breaking every low-flying discipline when flying over city centres.

It was a simple thing that brought every Nottingham dignitary to the airfield, awaiting the touchdown of the renegade aircraft. For, having booked a two-seater plane, when they arrived to commence their illicit sortie, there it was. But it wasn't the one booked – it had no floor-level loading bay, only side doors for the pilot and Les to climb aboard. The original plane they had booked had gone. Already on a tight schedule, there was no time for plan B. Even if they had a plan B, which apparently they didn't. What happened next was an unmitigated disaster.

On their very first low run over Nottingham's shopping centre, as Les upended the first sack of leaflets, almost half blew back into the cabin. As the pilot turned to commence his run back, the same thing happened. By now, there were more leaflets inside the aircraft than were drifting down onto the unsuspecting Nottingham shoppers. They were already well below the legal low-flying height, but by now the pilot's vision was badly impaired. He was clawing leaflets from his face and windscreen and this badly affected his control of the aircraft, now performing unwelcome aerobatics just a few hundred feet above hundreds of shoppers, all gazing heavenwards. The health and safety brigade was apoplectic. As Les started to empty sack number four, the aircraft started to climb and head for home – the pilot knew they were in serious trouble. Apart from breaking most of the rules governing low flying over major cities, his pilot's licence was now also in jeopardy. As they beat a hasty retreat, police cars were already arriving at the airport. The game was up, evidenced by the remaining large bags of leaflets still in the cockpit. Both were arrested, and, I believe, bailed to appear in court the following week. They had successfully alerted the citizens of Nottingham to the coming of the Kirchin band, greatly assisted by the unexpected national and local press coverage of Perrin's Peccadillos. Kirchin was over the moon. So pleased with the results achieved, he told Les he was permanently appointed as the band's publicist.

Legally, Les and his pilot companion were advised to plead guilty to all charges and expect a heavy fine. Knowing what lay ahead, he was further advised to withdraw from promoting the Moscow Dynamos tour, now just three weeks away. He did so there and then, leaving me stranded in Liverpool where the second tour game was due to be played.

Fortunately, there was expenses money enough to get me home to Kidbrooke, but I was out of work. Losing the job I was loving, plus the opportunity of a lifetime. I didn't know it then, but nor did Les. He wrote to me before his court appearance, explained what had happened and the disastrous effect the heavy fine expected would have on his new company. That he had no option, other than to dissolve it. He told me how sorry he was. Les died in 1978. Before he died, he worked with the Rolling Stones. By then, I would have been on his payroll. He as good as told me so.

Before appearing in court, he apologised profusely. He wished me well. Bitterly disappointed, I wished him dead.